WISDOM IN HUMOUR

WISDOM IN HUMOUR

Sri Swami Sivananda

Published By
THE DIVINE LIFE SOCIETY
P.O. SHIVANANDANAGAR—249 192
Distt. Tehri-Garhwal, Uttaranchal, Himalayas, India

Price]   2003   [Rs. 25/-

First Edition: 1951
Second Edition: 2003
(2,000 Copies)

©The Divine Life Trust Society

Published by Swami Jivanmuktananda for The Divine
Life Society, Shivanandnanagar, and printed by him
at the Yoga-Vedanta Forest Academy Press,
P.O. Shivanandanagar, Distt. Tehri-Garhwal,
Uttaranchal, Himalayas, India

PUBLISHERS' NOTE

(To the First Edition)

This Volume owes its birth to Sri Dr. Frederick Spiegelberg, professor of Stanford University, California, U.S.A., who was charmed when, at a Satsang held during his stay at Ananda Kutir in 1949, Sri Swami Sivanandaji Maharaj read out to him a few humorous compositions of his. "Swamiji!" said Dr. Frederick, "This is just the thing wanted by the people today. They would love the humour, but would unconsciously learn a spiritual lesson. The impression made by such teaching would be profound and lasting." This publication itself is a token of our gratitude to Dr. Frederick Spiegelberg.

Our grateful thanks ar due to Sri Swami Omkaranandaji for his invaluable help in collecting and editing the numerous poems written by Sri Swami Maharaj.

Ananda Kutir
20th February, 1951.   **Publishers**

CONTENTS

Publisher's Note v

CHAPTER I
VARIETIES IN WHIMS

1. Whims of Sadhus 15
2. Whims of Sadhakas 16
3. Varieties of Whims 18

CHAPTER II
OBJECTS SWEETER THAN BRAHMAN

1. Uppuma, Coffee, Is Sweeter than Brahman 20
2. Horrible Gluttons 21
3. English Laddu 21
4. Ode to Laddu 22

CHAPTER III
THE FRAILTY OF HUMAN LOVE

1. My Sweet Honey Darling 23
2. Woman's Crocodile's Tears 23

CHAPTER IV
HYPOCRITES

1. Do You Know this "I.C.S." & "P.C.S.?" 25
2. A Great F.F.S. and F.T.D. 25
3. Imitation Videhamukta 26
4. Here Is a Hypocrite 27
5. A Pseudo-Avadhooth 27
6. Pseudo-Patriots 28
7. Hypocritical Humility 29
8. A Deluded Soul 29
9. A Polished Cheat 30

CHAPTER V
THE MYSTERIOUS WORLD

1. This world—A mysterious show 31
2. Diverse Nature 31
3. Sounds and Bhava 32
4. Nature of Mundane Life 32
5. Discontentment Everywhere 33

CHAPTER VI
MORAL INSTRUCTIONS

1. Return Good for Evil 34
2. Tirupathi Shaving 34
3. Vritti-diseases 35
4. Fashionable Wife 35
5. Long Beard within a single Night 36
6. Do not Be Credulous 37
7. Fever Meets Itching 38
8. Tamper not with other's Letters 38
9. Hotel for Cats 39
10. Ladder, Teacher and Lemon-Pickle 39

CHAPTER VII
SPIRITUAL SERMONS

1. Khoon Kharab Hogaya 41
2. Your Wife Became a Widow 41
3. Preach to Yourself First 42
4. The Greatest Miser 42
5. Glory of Hotels! Rs. 30/- a Day 43
6. Poor Advocates 44
7. Dowry System 45
8. Story of a Miserly Millionaire 45
9. Story of Two Misers 46
10. Jagulee Chas, Bapulee Chas 46

11. Crush this Ego 47
12. World's Tallest Men 48
13. That Tomorrow Will never Come 48
14. Prosperious America 49
15. Ph.D. 49
16. March of India 50
17. Topics of the World 51
18. Three Kinds of Disciples 51
19. Story of a Pig 52
20. Boot-Legging 52
21. An Old Lady and a Needle 53
22. You Cannot Cheat the Indweller 53
23. Sunday Now Friday 54

CHAPTER VIII
A GUIDE TO DIVINE LIFE

1. Ek Niranjan; Do Gad Bhad; Teen Lat Pat 56
2. See the Lord in all Forms 56
3. The Frog and Faithless Disciples 57
4. Be Sincere and Aspire 57
5. Aspire for Liberation 58
6. Become a Doctor of Souls 59
7. Plants and Flowers 59
8. Milk, Dood, Pal and Ksheeram 60
9. Stages of Man 60
10. Do not Cheat 61
11. Eradicate Laziness 61
12. Seven Afflictions of a Pundit 62
13. Who Is a Sannyasi 62
14. Who Is A-1 "Loof" in Sirshasan? 63
15. Beard Is almost Equal to Gerua Cloth 63
16. Om Namo Narayanaya! 64
17. Sroty of a King's Cat 64

18. Sivaratri in E.I.R. 65
19. Story of a Cobra and a Farmer 66
20. The Modern Agnihotri 66
21. Snake-Rat Story 67
22. God Is Now Here 67
23. Look at Kallu's Devotion 68
24. Do Real Self-surrender 68
25. Dhanna Bhakta 69
26. Passion-Bye-Products 69
27. A Sadhu and a Seth 70
28. Chemo-Cherapy 71
29. Anti-Pneumo Thorax 71
30. Best Life Insurance Co. 72
31. Abandon Ownership 72
32. Pundit Ram with His Third Wife 73
33. Socrates and a Horse 73
34. Chaka Chak 74

CHAPTER IX
FALSE IMAGINATION

1. Vikalpa Vritti 75
2. Jiva Srishti Alone Gives Pain 75
3. Restless Horse-Mind 76
4. Effects of Dream 76
5. Mind Is like the Fountain Pen 77

CHAPTER X
VEDANTA IN HUMOUR

1. Dog in Stone 78
2. Sugar Cane Story 78
3. Atma Is Already There 79
4. Moorkhanandas 79
5. Sleepwalkers 80

6. The Tenth Was Missing 80
7. Properties of the Five Elements 81
8. Vedantic Bomb 81
9. Vedantic Gazette, Good News! 82
10. Vedantic Passport 83
11. Vedantic Suzerainty 83
12. Atma Bahadurs 84
13. U.N.O. 85
14. Solve this Riddle, Please 85
15. Shortage of Barbers 86

CHAPTER XI
VEDANTIC MEDICINES

1. Vedantic Beverage 87
2. Vedantic Compressed Tablet 87
3. Vedantic Vitamin 88
4. Vedantic TONIC 89

CHAPTER XII
LESSONS FROM SCIENTIFIC INVENTIONS

1. Television 90
2. Dicta-Hell—Tele 90
3. The Biggest Radio 91
4. Remove the Dirt in the Mind-Radio 91

CHAPTER XIII
HUMOROUS PIECES

1. Ear-complains to the Lord 93
2. To Lord Krishna 93
3. How to Become a Famous Sadhu 94
4. Tamarind Brain 94
5. Mixed Action 95
6. Ant, like the Atom Bomb 95
7. Elections and Voting 96

8. Twins and Triplets 96
9. Glory to Newspaper Boys 97
10. 'Procreate Less' Campaign 97
11. Husband and Wife 98
12. Three—Inches Intellect 98

CHAPTER XIV
SIVA'S NATIVE PLACE

1. Goodbye, Vain World 100
2. Song of Vibhuti Yoga 100
3. My Native Place 101
4. The Cow Tree 101
5. Intoximeter and Mayameter 102
6. Song of Honey 103
7. Digambara Song 103
8. Ram Kirtan 103
9. That Divine Whisky 104
10. Nature Curist Is Intolerant 104
11. Nature Curist Vrittis 105
12. Allopathic Monsters 105
13. Naturopath's Poor Prarabdha 106
14. The Family of Egoism 106
15. The Best 106
16. Lecture By Milk 107
17. Son of Asanas 108
18. Incompatibles 111

SECTION II
PHILOSOPHY IN HUMOUR

1. To Lord Krishna 112
2. Maya 112
3. Daya Krishna and Danveer Ram 114
4. "Tor" Ka "Dur" 116

5. Story of Ade-Vada 116
6. Spiritual Smoking 119
7. Story of Dosai Sangam 122
8. Philosophy of Beard 124
9. Pseudo-Vedantin 126
10. Impotent Vedantin 127
11. Lip Vedantin 129
12. Real Vedantin 130
13. Divine Injection S.B. 40 131
14. Spiritual Lumbago 131
15. The Knowledge of the Lad 133
16. Best Cement 134
17. Fountain Pen 134
18. Knowledge of a Child 135
19. Boy Becomes a Girl 136
20. Moustache Lady 137
21. Test-tube Baby 138
22. Spiritual Shaving 138
23. Chandrabhaga and Monkey 142
14524. A Complaint to Brahma 145
25. The Story of a Laddu 145
26. The Secret of "Bada" 146
27. This Is Maya 146
28. Philosophy of Shirt and Hat 148
29. Equal Vision 149
30. Gadapparai or Durmat Nyaya 150
31. Brahma-Jnana Research Pharmacy 150
32. Tat Tvam Asi 151
33. Recipe (Take Thou) 151
34. Philosophy of Proverbs 152
35. The Maha Kumbha Mela 159
36. Wake Up O! Man 168

WISDOM IN HUMOUR

WISDOM IN HUMOUR

CHAPTER 1

VARIETIES IN WHIMS

1. WHIMS OF SADHUS

One Sadhu will not touch money,
But he wants a treasurer to carry the money.
Another does not wish to use a blanket:
He considers himself to be a great Vairagi;
But he wants heaps of dried straw.
He enters into it like a horizontal being and uses
a straw pillow:
This is another kind of whim of a Sadhu.
He can just ward off cold by using a small blanket.
He regards himself to be a great Tyagi
By giving up blanket and pillow.
Pundit Madan Mohan Malaviya took with him
A Sannyasin to Mussorie.
It was raining in torrents.
The Sannyasin used to sleep in a bed of grass.
He wanted straw and straw alone as his bed.
Panditji said, "It is difficult to get straw here.
It is raining heavily now.
Please use this cot and blankets today."
The Swamiji said, "No, no, no, I want grass only."
A bundle of grass was brought with great difficulty.
This is another whim.
One Sadhu walks naked in the street,
But keeps few blankets in his Kutir.
Attachment to Vairagya is as much an evil
As attachment to Raga itself.
Whims of Sadhus are beyond description.
They are diverse, curious and ludicrous.
Practise intelligent Tapas,
And be a sensible Sadhu or Swami.

2. WHIMS OF SADHAKAS

Some concentrate their Sadhana on hair;
Some apply ash and make it golden;
Some shave the head completely;
Some keep Jata or matted hair;
Some keep long hair;
Some have "modified crop";
They all have their hair
Under perfect control.
Some have long beard.
They apply oil and comb it daily.
They think that a beard
Will give a good personality,
Make them appear saintly and Yogily,
And bring respect from all quarters.
This is their hair (or Mair) Sadhana.
Their minds assume hair-akara Vritti:
Their minds are ever fixed on hair.
This is their goal, centre and Ideal.
They make the body Brahman or a saint.
They cheat themselves and others too.
Their hands are ever on their beard.
Watch carefully, you will agree with me.
Some do Kowpeen or langot Sadhana.
Today they will wear gerrua gown or orange *alphe*.
Tomorrow they will put on
A short cloth above the knee;
Next day they will have only one Kowpeen.
The following day they will roam about stark naked.
They think they have realised the Avadhut state
Of possessionlessness and perfect non-attachment,
But their minds remain in the same state
Or even in a worse state,
Because their egoism is intensified now;
Their veil of ignorance is thickened
By this sort of Tapas.
They think that they are superior Sadhakas.
Now comes nim-leaves-buttermilk Sadhana.

VARIETIES IN WHIMS

Some live on nim leaves for a month;
Some drink cow's urine;
Some leave salt and sugar,
They take buttermilk today;
They live tomorrow on vegetables.
They live next day on ground nuts;
They live the following day on Sattu.
They observe Mouna, say 'Ha', 'Hu', 'Hu', 'O'.
They talk more than worldly men.
Cultivate 'Mitha Bashan', a little useful talking.
Next comes Sadhana in Himalayas.
Some live in Gangotri;
Some live in Caves;
Some live in Uttarakashi;
Some live in Lonely forests;
Some live in Mount Kailas;
Some live in Mansarowar.
They think they have realised Brahman.
But their nature remains the same
Or becomes even worse,
On account of a little Tapas Abhiman.
Their quarrelling and arrogant nature
Becomes more marked.
Their egoism is more hard than granite.
They wander about advertising
That they are Jivanmuktas.
They repeat Sivoham, Soham.
Little things upset them,
And make them "Durvasa".
They now begin to start "Ashrams",
And open "Dharma Sanghas",
To do Lokasangraha.
Taking nim, remaining naked, keeping beard,
Is the gist of their whole Sadhana.
Their Sadhana ends with these only.
They think of buttermilk, beard,
Kowpeen, cave and Gangotri.
Due to under nutrition and exposure,

They contract chronic diseases,
And die an early unnatural death.
They miss their life's goal.
They never think of the Eternal.
This is all due to their 'Manmukh nature,
They have not done any "Gurumukh Sadhana"
Keeping a beard cannot make one a Jnani.
Eating nim leaves cannot make one a Yogi.
Giving up salt cannot open the Kundalini.
Salt, sugar and both are not obstacles to Brahma Jnana.
Kings were in possession of Brahma Jnana.
Remaining naked cannot make one an Avadhoot
Purify the mind, reduce the egoism to zero.
Live under a Guru and practise Sadhana
Serve the poor, regenerate the Asuric nature
Eat anything that comes by chance
Do not make any show of your saintliness.
Be steady, firm, normal and uniform.
Abandon eccentricity and queer nature,
Never give up selfless service.
Do not jump to the skies at once
Shave the mind and burn the Vasanas and
                                    Dambhachariness
Be mentally silent and yet dynamic
And waft the divine aroma everywhere
Hari OM, Sri OM, Siva OM, Ram OM.

3. VARIETIES OF WHIMS

One Sadhu wears stockings, head turban and coat
But he leaves his private parts exposed.
One Sadhu moves about with Kowpeen only
But he keeps fountain pen, covers and cards;
He lives in Mt. Kailas for 3 months
And moves from door to door in the plains for 9 months.
One Sadhu wears a tiger skin only
But he goes to Maharajahs for collection of money.
One Sadhu wears only one cloth at a time.
If he wears a blanket, he gives his Langoti to his disciple;

VARIETIES IN WHIMS

If he wears a Langoti, then he gives his blanket.
Some keep beards to get respect: "OM Namo Narayanaya."
Some keep beards to have a good personality.
Some are extreme Viraktas.
But they cannot pull on without coffee, tiffin,
mtobacco and betels.
There must be a meaning on your Tapas:
Householders are more intelligent than the Sadhus.
They can at once find out their motives.
If you are a real Virakta, do not enter the plains.
Why do you want pen, coffee and newspapers?
Why do you write articles?
Do not keep notes or sovereigns in your Kowpeen.
Be true; be sincere; be a real Sadhu.

CHAPTER II

OBJECTS SWEETER THAN BRAHMAN

1. "UPPUMA, COFFEE, IS SWEETER THAN BRAHMAN!"

A Madrasi says:
"Your Brahman is not so sweet
As my Uppuma, Sambhar and coffee."
A Maharashtra says:
" Your Atman is not delicious
As my *Varana. Amte* and *Poornapoli*."
A Punjabi declares:
"Your Vedantic Brahman is not so palatable
As my Parotta, milk and Sag."
A Gujarathi says
"Your Upanishadic Atman is not so sweet
As my Kadhi, Laddhu and tea."
A Bengali asserts:
"Your Brahman is not so delicious
As my Rasagulla and Sandesh."
A European proclaims:
"Your Brahman is not so sweet
As my beef-steak, sweet pudding and dripping."
Maya is very powerful.
It deludes, tricks and dupes,
It makes unreal appear as real
And hides the Real.
Maya makes the objects appear
More sweet than Brahman
In order to deceive the worldlings.
Any amount of lecturing and tuition
Cannot open the eyes of these people.
They are immersed and soaked in worldliness 1001 deep!
Pain—deep and continuous—and knocks of this world
Satsang, discrimination and enquiry

At last open their eyes,
They act as wisdom collyrium.

2. HORRIBLE GLUTTONS

There are many horrible gluttons in this world.
They load their stomach like the Railway trucks.
Go to Muttra and see the Chaubais.
They eat one cartload of Pedas with Bhang.
These gluttons cannot stand erect
After this overloading.
They fall down on the earth straight,
And start snoring instantaneously.
Their bellies are like huge machines.
Such gluttons are burdens on this earth.
O man! give up gluttony
Gluttony produces various diseases.
It makes one forget God.
Be moderate in eating.
A glutton is an object of ridicule.
Sing, pray and meditate,
And attain God-realisation quickly.

3. ENGLISH LADDU

Europeans like this laddu immensely,
They die for this laddu.
They eat this avidity, cupidity and stupidity
Brahmin children throw this away.
Some Indians also take this laddu
                with the same avidity and stupidity.
Its shape is different from Hindu laddu.
Its colour is different,
Its composition also is different.
Its property also is different.
This laddu is Tamasic.
It hinders meditation.
It is an enemy of Naturopaths.
It cannot be broken lengthwise.
It is not man-make laddu.
This famous English laddu is Anda or egg.

4. ODE TO LADDU

O Laddu! O Sweet laddu!
Adorations unto thee!
Thou art the pet child of Maya:
You delude the people to a great degree,
Children dance in joy when they look at you,
Even old people jump and whistle.
Last night the Bhajan Hall
Was packed with people
Because there was laddu Prasad.
Jeelabhi, Peda, Rasagulla; Kalakand,
Are thy amiable companions
But people like you only most
I do not know what charms are in these.
This world will be a void minus thee.
You hold a very prominent position
In Bhandaras, feasts and diners
Even diabetics fill their stomachs with Laddus
On the strength of Insulin.
Thou art very dear to Muttra Chaubais,
Even dysenteric patients cannot leave thee,
They do not mind aggravation of the disease.
You are only a modification of mud and water,
And yet how powerful thou art!
You hold sway over all,
You put down your head in shame
Before sages, devotees and Yogis,
Because they know your hollowness.
Goodbye, laddu, amiable comrade,
Continue the work vigorously
And delude the worldly weaklings intensely.

CHAPTER III

THE FRAILITY OF HUMAN LOVE

1. MY SWEET HONEY DARLING

The wife says to the husband at night
"O my sweet honey! O my darling!!
O my sweet-heart! how I love you!!
I cannot live without you even for a second:
Thou art the apple of my eye,
Thou art my very Prana (life),
I will pine away if I do not see you even for a second."
The husband also repeats the same phrases,
Perhaps, even with greater force.
But the following morning
She may divorce her husband without a moment's notice;
He also may divorce her within a minute.
Such is the nature of human love
It is hollow, shallow, fleeting like the lightning
It is mixed with cunningness, crookedness and selfishness.
There is no real love in this world.
Develop pure, divine love towards God
And rest in Him peacefully for ever.

2. WOMAN'S CROCODILE'S TEARS

Woman is a weakling
She is not so strong as man.
But she is cunning and sheds tears quickly;
Her lachrymal gland is ever in a state to irritation.
It is ever ready with gallons of tears.
These are her weapons to accomplish her objects.
Poor husband is deluded!
He is carried away by her tears.
He yields and bends to her will.
He says:" Darling, today I shall give orders
For the necklace, bangles and silk saree."
O chicken-hearted man: Rise from impotence.

Do not be swept away by woman's crocodile's tears.
This is her trick and cunningness.
Be strong; be not effeminate.
Stick to your principles and ideals.
No one has been benefited by Maya.
Believe her not quickly.
She is very, very deep.
Even her husband who lives with her for 40 years
Cannot sound the depths of her heart.
Wipe away lust which makes you cling
                          to a woman like a leech,
Which has weakened your will,
And merge in the blissful Atman.

CHAPTER IV

HYPOCRITES

1. DO YOU KNOW THIS "I.C.S.& P.C.S.?"

One man puts his title as M.Bh.
This is not a doctor's title;
It means only "Madras Brahmin".
One man has his title S.S.O.
It is not a sub-divisional officer;
It means, "Simply Sitting Officer,"
That is an idler, loafer or a Faltu.
One man uses the title, M.R.K.D.,
It means "Member of the
Rice killing Department" or
Rotti Killing Department',
That is "a glutton or *Sapatraman*",
Who fills his belly with rice or rotti upto mouth.
Another calls himself I.C.S. in summer
And P.C.S. in winter;
It means Ice-Cream Seller in summer,
And Potatoe Chop Seller in winter.
Such title holders are plenty in this world.
Please do not aspire to own
Such big title and come to limelight.
Shun all such title, hide yourself;
You will be peaceful.
Sincerity, simplicity, humility,
Generosity and devotion to God,
These you should own and not
Self-deluding and world-cheating titles
Of the above type.

2. A GREAT F.F.S. & F.T.D.

One man applied for a Head Master's Post;
He had passed only third Form,
But he put his titles as F.F.S., F.T.D.

The Trustees of the High School
Were enamoured of his big titles;
They appointed him as the Head Master.
The Head Master worked for a week;
He was not able to deliver lectures,
The students pressed him to deliver lectures,
But the Head Master blinked.
The Trustees asked, "What are these titles, then?"
You are not able to deliver lectures
He said "I am Father of Five Sons, 'F.F.S.'
And father of ten daughters,' F.T.D.!"
The trustees said, "Get away at once,
Oh! cheat, we do not want you."
This world abounds with cheats.
Beware, be cautious, be vigilant.
Do not be carried away by titles, F.F.S.F.T.D.
America issues very cheap titles.
Egoistic man wants titles,
To pose as a big man in this world.
Be simple, humble, do not cheat.

3. IMITATION VIDEHAMUKTA

You have imitation silk.
You have imitation diamond.
Even so, you have imitation Videhamukta,
Or pseudo Videhamukta.
This man also throws away all clothes:
Sometimes passes motion in his seat.
He is fed by others,
Who belong to the same gang or community.
They have got alternate duties.
Today Swami Ram will sit like Videhamukta.
Tomorrow the turn will come to Swami Krishnananda.
This is a very big company or big business.
The hot charcoal test
And the Bitchu Katta Buttee test
Will surely open the eyes
Of these imitation Videhamuktas.

Some are not imitation Videhamuktas.
They are very good, sincere souls, indeed;
But they foolishly imagine
That they have attained this Videhamukti stage
By simply reading Yoga-Vashishta
And doing a little Sadhana,
And having a vision of colours and lights—
What is seen is not Atman.

4. HERE IS A HYPOCRITE

He has nothing to eat in the house;
But he wears spectacles and holds a silver-plated stick;
He wears a silk shirt, earrings and golden chain;
He does not know the alphabet;
Bur he keeps a newspaper in his hand and a big book;
Here is a hypocrite.
He does not know what is Yama, Niyama and Dhyana.
But he cuts his tongue, keeps a Yoga Danda,
Proclaims that he practises "Khechari Mudra",
And says "That Judge is my disciple: This Raja is my Chela".
Here is a first class or capital hypocrite.
He does not know anything of Vedanta.
He has not even an iota of "Sadhana Chatushtaya";
But he keeps a Kamandalu, shaves his head,
Repeats always "Sivoham, Sivoham",
And proclaims, "I am a Jivanmukta in the Turiya."
He is an A. I. confirmed hypocrite!
Believe him not, approach him not,
Shun him at a distance and be free.

5. A PSEUDO AVADHOOTH

Avadooths are naked Sanyasins.
They do not wear any cloth or keep any vessel.
They take their Bhiksha in their hands.
Some times people feed them in the mouth.
Maharani Pratap Kumari was a pious woman,
She used to feed Avadhoots in their mouth,
One day a Pseudo Avadhoot came to the palace.
He thought he also would enjoy nicely.

The Maharani found him out.
She had great experience of Mahatmas.
She could discriminate "who is who?"
She mixed some nim paste in the sweetmeat.
She gave him first fruits and milk.
Afterwards she gave him this sweetmeat.
The pseudo Avadhooth became very angry
And abused the Maharani and went away.
Beware of pseudo Avadhooths.
They keep several blankets in their Kutirs.

6. PSEUDO PATRIOTS

A man puts on a Gandhi cap
And wears thick Khaddar.
He bawls out, Mahatma Gandhiji ki-Jai"
He thinks he is a great patriot.
He does not possess any good qualities
That make up a real patriot.
Another man condemns "English speaking',
He is a very intolerant man;
He says to every one:
"Speak Hindustani. Do not speak in English".
He thinks he is a great patriot.
A few months ago
He was cramming English passages;
He took great pride in talking in English;
He talked in English even to his old ignorant mother;
He had a newspaper and an English book in his hand;
He wanted to get a good job.
Even orthodox Sanskrit Pandits learn English.
Because he can get Rs 80/-in the High School
Instead of Rs. 30/-only.
Boys from India running to America and England
To prosecute higher studies.
Can they manage without English?
English in India can never die.
Be tolerant, friend?
English also is born of OM.

7. HYPOCRITICAL HUMILITY

Hypocritical humility is dangerous.
It is trained vanity or pride.
It is developed crookedness and cunningness.
It is a systematic or well-organised cheating,
It is concentrated diplomacy.
It is pride in essence.
A man of hypocritical humility
Will be detected soon by intelligent people.
He pretends to be what he is not.
Like a trained actor,
He makes some studied gestures and movements
For the time being
He shows his teeth, bends his neck and sits on the ground;
At other times he manifests his own nature.
He is like a tiger in cow's clothing.
Real humility is artless and uniform.
It is innocent, elevating and inspiring.
It is magnetic force, a divine attribute.
Be really humble and become divine.

8. A DELUDED SOUL.

An American from Santa Barbara came to me.
He knows several Asanas.
He wanted initiation from me.
I gave him Brahmacharya Diksha in white cloth.
He went to another Swami after some days.
And put on gerrua cloth or orange-coloured robe.
He lived in Brahmapuri forest for 20 days.
He came out and declared
"I have seen Lord Krishna.
I have attained God-realisation".
Somebody asked the American:
"What did Lord Krishna say to you?"
He replied: "He asked me to go to America."
Is God realisation so cheap and so easy?
People have no idea of God-realisation.

The world abounds with such deluded souls.
Do not believe them; do not be duped.

9. A POLISHED CHEAT

To all appearance he is more than a Saint;
He is very sweet in his speech,
Polished in his manners and conduct;
He is generous, he serves people,
He gives presents, he bows and is courteous,
Nobody will suspect him.
He speaks a few words,
He is a thorough gentleman every inch.
He closely watches for opportunities,
Then he drags his sword and slowly cuts the throat;
He swindles in a thorough, wholesale manner.
Nobody can detect his swindling.
He is an accomplished expert in this line
He is a Presidency first M.A. In this art.
This is a very strange world, friend.
Be careful, be vigilant, be cautious.
Do not place full trust on all.
Beware of polished, dangerous cheats.

CHAPTER V

THE MYSTERIOUS WORLD

1. THIS WORLD—A MYSTERIOUS SHOW

Some Rajahs take delight
In having a hospital and zoo for dogs,
In arranging marriages for them!
And in taking these dogs in procession!!
Some take great pleasure
In breading good horses and making money.
Some train cocks and bulls for fighting.
Some train hawks for fight.
Some are fond of hunting, "Shikar".
Some are great Cricketers.
Some start cinema studios.
Some revel in harems "three-hundred-strong".
Some collect specimen of womanhood from each nation!
Some go for pilgrimage to Kailas.
Some start Sanskrit Colleges.
Some write books.
Some do Japa and Meditation.
This world is a mysterious show of God.
People have different fancies.
They reap the fruits
According to their fancies and deeds.

2. DIVERSE NATURE

An I.C.S. officer had four sons.
One son had a taste for music;
Another had a taste for cricket;
A third had a taste for poetry.
One son became a doctor;
Another son became an Engineer;
A third became a Professor;
The fourth son was a dunce.
How do you account for all these differences?

Why was the fourth son a dunce,
When he, too, had all favourable conditions
                              and environment?
Each son had his own Karmas,
                    impressions and predilections.
He carried them from his previous birth.
Each one had his own mental make up.
No two minds agree in this world.
Diversity is the nature of Prakriti.

3. SOUNDS AND BHAVA

Recitation of Vedic hymns elevates the mind,
'Bum', 'Bum' of Ganga fixes the mind,
Music, Raga-Raginees, Soothes the mind;
Jarring sounds disturb the mind.
Kind words create friendship;
Harsh words produce enemity.
Chanting of Om and other Mantras
Generate Sattvic Bhava and peace of mind
And bring the aspirant face to face with God.
Bija Askhara sounds give strength.
Words like fool, dunce, son of a bitch,
Sala, throw a man into explosive fury;
Words like Maharaj Prabhu, Hon. Sir,
Give great satisfaction and exhilaration.

4. NATURE OF MUNDANE LIFE.

Mundane life is full of sorrows, pains and bondage.
It is full of defects, weaknesses and limitations.
It is full of hatred, jealousy, selfishness, treachery,
Care, worries, anxieties, disease and death,
Meanness, crookedness, deceit, double-dealing,
Cut-throat competition, impurities and darkness,
Fights, quarrels, strife and war,
Disappointment, despair and dejection,
Cruelty, exploitation, agitation, restlessness.
All objects are coated with a little imaginary pleasure;
It is like a thin electro-gold plating.
In reality, life here is all tinsel and shadow.

Behind the sugar-coating there is bitter Quinine;
Behind the gold-electro plating it is all brass.
Behind the so-called pleasure there are pain,
                              misery and suffering.
Life here is full of fears, attachments and tribulations.
Beware! Wake up! Seek the Immortal Bliss within your Soul.

5. DISCONTENTMENT EVERYWHERE

The Sessions Judge is very discontented,
He thirsts to become a High Court Judge;
The Minister is also discontented,
He longs to become the Premier;
A millionaire is discontented,
He yearns to become a croropati;
The husband is discontented,
His wife is black and thin,
He wants to marry another wife with good complexion;
The wife is discontented,
She wants to divorce and marry a rich, young husband.
A lean man is discontented,
He wants to put on fat and gulps codliver oil;
A fat man is discontented,
He wants to reduce his fat and takes anti-fat pills;
No man is contented in this world,
Real, eternal, satisfaction comes only
Through attainment of the All-full Atman.
Therefore, realise this Self-contained, Paripoorna, Self.

CHAPTER VI
MORAL INSTRUCTIONS

1. RETURN GOOD FOR EVIL

A cow killed a bee with its tail.
A swarm of bees of about 60,000
Stung the cow to death,
Leaving 10,000 casualities of their own.
This happened Tohira, Japan.
Revenge is deep-rooted in all creatures.
It is manifestation of deep hatred.
Hatred is the enemy of wisdom and peace.
Remove hatred through love and enquiry.
Revenge not, but return good for evil,
You will reap a rich harvest of everlasting peace.

2. TIRUPATHI SHAVING

In Tirupathi a barber is very busy;
His clients are countless.
Children and elders shave their heads.
This is considered a very auspicious
The barber shaves a little portion at first,
He does not want to lose his client;
He collects a large number,
Then he begins to shave one by one neatly.
A tailor, even when he has very tight work,
Will not refuse to undertake the work of anybody;
He will simply collect work from all corners.
And will give lame excuses daily.
When he sees a man
He will pretend to take up the work
And cut a small portion and stitch;
When the man leaves his shop,
He will take up another work.
Even so, some take up my letters
And, after five or six days, say.

MORAL INSTRUCTIONS

"I have kept the reply on the table.
Yes, Narayana Swami has taken that letter.
No, no, it is with Premananda;
No, no, it is with Atma Ram in the Post Office."
In reality the letter is somehow lost,
Be not like the barber or tailor:
Take up any work and finish it promptly,
Give not this and that lame excuse,
Stick to your promise.

3. VRITTI-DISEASES

The root-cause of all diseases is ignorance.
Desire is rheumatism.
Greed is phlegm.
Anger is bile.
These torture the heart.
"When all these three attack you,
You are a prey to pneumonia fever.
Mineness is the ringworm.
Jealousy is the scratching itch.
Raga is the throat's cancer.
Envy is the incurable T.B.
Malice is leprosy.
Egoism is gout.
Pride, hypocrisy, are neuritis.
Hatred is malignant malaria.

4. FASHIONABLE WIFE

Such a wife is a great nuisance.
She always quarrels with her husnand.
She squanders money.
She sends money to her parents, brothers and sisters.
This creates more trouble in the house.
She is never contented.
She wastes money in Sarees and necklaces.
She cannot cook.
She wants several servants,
She quarrels with them;
The servants go away.

Where to get new, new, servants?
The husband is puzzled and worried.
When he sits for meditation.
She thinks that he will take Sannyasa soon.
She quarrels with him on this score.
The house, "Rama Vilas" or "Shanti Villa",
Is a terrible hell, indeed.
If you ask her to bring a cup of tea,
If she is annoyed,
Because you did not carry out
Her wish for a diamond necklace,
She will say,
"You are a graduate,
I am also a graduate;
bring me a cup of tea first'.
Be careful in selecting your wife.
There must be psychological unity;
She must be religious and pious.
Select your wife from country girls
To whom modern civilisation and radio
Have not penetrated.

5. LONG BEARD WITHIN A SINGLE NIGHT

Ram was is the habit of taking bhang.
He went to a shop at 10 p.m
And asked for almonds for annas eight.
He threw one rupee on the desk.
The shopkeeper said, "O man! I am closing the shop now,
Come tomorrow morning".
Ram replied, "I want to satisfy my craving now".
The shopkeeper gave Ram almonds.
He did not return annas eight as he had no change.
Ram took the almonds and came back.
There was a bull in front of the shop.
He took this as a mark to recognise the shop.
In the next morning he went to the shop.
To get back his eight annas.
The bull was found in front of a tailor's shop.

Ram asked the shopkeeper to return his eight annas.
The shopkeeper said, "I did not have any
                                    transaction with you."
Ram said, "It is all Kali, you are telling a lie;
But how is it you have developed such a long beard
Within a single night for the sake of eight annas?"

6. DO NOT BE CREDULOUS

A Sadhu had biliousness.
He vomited some black matter.
The news went out quickly
That the Sadhu had vomited a black crow.
A householder invited a Sadhu for Bhiksha.
The mistress of the house by mistake
Put salt instead of sugar in the Kheer.
The Sadhu took all the salted Kheer quietly.
He did not utter even a single word.
The news went out that the Sadhu converted
                                    the salt into sugar.
Sadhu asked his disciple to bring some fried gram.
He said "Keep this with you.
I will take after two hours when it become laddu".
After two hours the Sadhu said,
"O disciple, I am very hungry, bring the laddu".
The disciple replied, "It still remains as gram only.
It has not been converted into laddu".
The Sadhu said, "As I am very hungry now
The gram will be more than laddu to me now".
The news reached everywhere
That the Sadhu converted the gram into laddu.
Such is the world.
One thing occurs, it is exaggerated,
                            transformed and twisted
In all the Newspapers next morning.
Do not be credulous.
Think, reflect and discriminate
And take the essence, the Truth.

7. FEVER MEETS ITCHING

Bookar meets Kujlee.
A Bania (Merchant) had fever.
He fasted on seven occasions,
The fever left him.
A Jat (Labourer, athlete) had itching.
He applied ash of dried plantain leaves,
Rubbed the skin vigorously with the ash,
Itching left him instantaneously.
Now fever of Bania and Itching of Jat met.
Fever said; "Who are you?"
"I am fever that left the Bania;
Let us exchange our abode."
Itching came and dwelt in the body of Bania comfortably,
Bania applied oil to his body,
So itching could comfortably dwell in his body.
He can afford and has ample time for scratching.
He can scratch with one hand
And write the ledger with the other hand.
He cannot apply rough ash to his body like the Jat.
Fever came and dwelt comfortably in the Jat.
The Jat did daily Dand and Baitak exercises,
Even though there was fever.
The fever increased after the daily exercises.
Have a strong, enduring, frame.
Abandon ease and comfort.
Have a rough and hard skin
That can stand against heat and cold.

8. TAMPER NOT WITH OTHER'S LETTERS

In 1923 one man in Chicago
Was charged with opening a letter
Addressed to his wife,
Whom he suspected of "carrying on"
With another man.
The Judge declared:
"You tampered with the mails.

I sentenced you to 25 seconds' imprisonment."
The Judge took the watch and counted the seconds.
When he reached "Twentyfive",
The prisoner was released from custody.
Tampering with the letters of others is a crime.
It is against decorum and decent conduct.

9. HOTEL FOR CATS

Miss Rachel Loveday has opened
A hotel for cats in a wing of her house
In Beckenham, Kent.
The guests are cats belonging to neighbours
Who are away temporarily.
She charges only the rich.
There is a drawing room for cats with armchairs.
These cats ought to have been men in their previous birth.
Thanks to Miss Rachel.
Here is a field for her for developing compassion.
Cats are also manifestations of Lord Hari.
Cultivate divine bhava while serving cats.
She must have small dispensary
And an indoor hospital, too, with at least two beds.
O Usha, O Uma, will you also open a cat's hotel here?

10. LADDER, TEACHER AND LEMON PICKLE

The ladder and staircase help people
To go up and enjoy the scenery;
But they remain in the same position.
A teacher helps students to rise up
They become collectors, Judges and doctors;
But he remains in the same state
As an ordinary school master drawing Rs. 25/-.
Lemon pickle helps a man
To digest anything and everything;
But it itself remains undigested.
The ladder and the stair case
The teacher and the lemon pickle

Were grumbling and discontented;
They all repaired to Ananda Kutir
And made a complaint to the Swami.
Swami said: "Your professions are all noble.
Be contented with doing good to others."
They became silent and rejoiced heartily.

CHAPTER VII

SPIRITUAL SERMONS

1. KHOON KHARAB HOGAYA

When the blood is full and thick
The young man jumps and dances
Twists his moustache and denies God:
It is all "I did this", "I know everything".
"No one is equal to me. I can do anything'.
He drinks, gambles, plays all mischief,
Gets various sorts of diseases,
Then comes to the doctor and says
"Doctor Sahib, Khoon Kharb Hogaya,"
And takes 606 and 914 injections.
His face is pale now;
He walks with tottering steps;
He hides his face in shame;
He drags a cheerless existence.
O Man! when you are full blooded
Think of God, be good and do good.
Walk in the path of righteousness;
Approach the saints and follow their instructions;
You will reap a rich harvest of peace.

2. YOUR WIFE BECAME A WIDOW

Once a man went to receive a friend of his
At the Railway station on his arrival after a long time.
The friend on meeting him enquired
Whether all his friends and relatives are well.
The man replied, "Yes, all are well
But there is only one sad news, and
That is, your wife recently became a widow."
As his friend was a simple and artless man,
He began to weep very bitterly
And beat his breasts severely.
Then the man explained to his friend,

"Do not be foolish, O Ram.
How can your wife become a widow when you are alive?"
Thereupon he gained strength slowly.
Such is the delusion of the worldling!
He takes this perishable body as the immortal soul
And creates all sorts of "mine-ness";
He weeps on account of Moha.
The merciful sage consoles him
And gives him instructions:
"O man, you are not this mortal body
You are in essence Satchidananda Svaroopa;
Wake up from the slumber of ignorance;
"Tat Twam Asi", "That thou art".
Thereupon He gains spiritual strength,
Meditates and attains self-realisation.

3. PREACH TO YOURSELF FIRST

The dry Pundit stands on the pulpit
And delivers high-sounding lectures.
But he himself is a spiritual bankrupt.
But knows how to prattle, or Jalpa,
And excite or dupe the credulous and the ignorant.
He has crammed some passages and phrases at night.
He vomits them in the morning.
He moves about aimlessly.
He feels highly elevated by applause.
O pundit! O lecturer! O preacher!
Preach or lecture to yourself first.
Have you got any real knowledge to give to the hearers?
Have you got any strength to lift up others?
Be not like the blind leading the blind.
Yourself and the hearers will both fall into the deep abyss.

4. THE GREATEST MISER

In Manasic Pooja or mental worship
You can offer anything to the Lord,
You can offer the sweetmeats of the whole world,
The fruits of the entire universe,
The gold and rubies of all mines,

The clothes of the whole world.
But one devotee offered in his mental worship
One stale plantain only and one teaspoonful of
                              green gram only!
Is he not the greatest miser?
If he is such a sort of miser even in mental
                              offering to the Lord,
How can one expect even a grain of rice from him?
He will not give even a little salt to a man
                              with a cut in the finger.
He will not drive the crows when he is taking food
Lest a grain of rice might fall on the ground
Which the crow might get!!.
Such misers are a burden on this earth.
O man! Develop a generous heart.
Give, give, give, always give.
This is the secret of abundance.
You will inherit the whole wealth of the Lord.
You will be ever full.
Dhana Lakshmi, Dhanya Lakshmi, will ever dwell in you.

5. GLORY OF HOTELS!! Rs. 30/-A DAY

In Savoy Hotel, Mussoorie,
You will have to pay Rs. 14/- daily.
In Imperial Hotel, Delhi,
You will have to pay Rs. 25/- daily.
In Taj Mahal Hotel, Bombay,
You will have to pay Rs. 30/- daily.
If you want a special drawing-room also,
You will have to pay Rs. 80/- daily.
You will have all sorts of comforts;
Hot-water tap, cold-water tap, etc.
There are dancing, band-playing, during meals.
Very lovely and beautiful, indeed!!!
There are all sorts of materials,
To excite all your senses to their climax,
To make you forget God and Truth completely.
There is beauty competition among males and females

Through votes.
A rich man presides.
Males vote for the most beautiful woman.
Females vote for the most handsome man.
They get prizes too—diamond rings, etc.
There are dinner, dancing and drinking.
The woman who gets the first prize
Is invited for dinners by rich men.
She is ruined miserably here and there.
Hotels are centres of mayaic play.
All sorts of temptations are here.
Men and women are entrapped here.
All sorts of things go on here.
O men and women! Who revel in filth,
And so have become vermins!
Who do not practice Japa, meditation and Vichara;
Regain your lost divinity;
Be pious, God-fearing and religious.
There is yet hope for you all.
Attain immortal bliss through self-purification,
Self-restraint, self-analysis and meditation.

6. POOR ADVOCATES

Advocates do Japa daily
Of "Your Worship", "Your Honour" and "My Lord".
When they plead before the Magistrate or Munsif,
They address him "Your Worship",
When they plead before the district judge,
They address him "Your Honour";
When they plead before the High Court Judge,
They address him "My Lord".
If they daily address the Lord with these terms,
Who dwells in the chamber of their heart,
They would have become great devotees by this time.
O advocates! Who dance in the courts
For the sake of this belly,
Dance and sing Kirtan before the Lord,

You will obtain the immortal bread.
That makes you hungerless and deathless.

7. DOWRY SYSTEM

This must vanish immediately.
The boy threatens his father-in-law;
"I will send my wife to your house;
You have not given me a proper dowry.
You have not given me silver vessels,
Money for higher education in England,
Silk-clothes and valuable wrist-watch".
He sends back his wife to his father-in-law's house.
If one has twelve daughters like our Mr. Rao,
He must perish quickly.
Marriage has become a good business.
It is not a sacred sacrament now.
O man! practise Langot Bandha and Kowpeen Mudra,
You will have peace of mind.
O Law Ministers! Stop this system at once.
Dowry system is a blot on India's fame.

8. STORY OF A MISERLY MILLIONAIRE

Joseph Bowling, 75, of New Jersey, U.S.A.
Ate a Rs. 2-11-0 meal per day
Till he died of starvation recently
With Rs. 16, 17,000 in the bank.
He worked for 25 years in the Income-tax division.
His clothes were ragged and filthy.
He lived in a 1.50 dollar per night room.
He ate only one meal a day.
He never spoke to any one.
He died of malnutrition in a hospital.
His wealth was found out by his brother
After Bowling was buried as a pauper.
This is the fate of all misers!
O misers! Make good use of your money.
Construct hospitals, Sanskrit colleges.
Yoga Ashrams, Orphanages, Public Libraries,
Research Institutions and Universities,

And enter the Kingdom of eternal bliss
Through meritorious deeds.

9. STORY OF TWO MISERS

One miser, Rama, was eating bread.
He simply touched the ghee a little bit.
The other miser, Krishna, hung the tin of ghee
On a nail above.
He looked at it and ate the bread.
Rama thought that Krishna was more clever than he,
Because there was not a bit of decrease in his ghee.
He also followed the example of Krishna.
Two monkeys came now
And snatched the ghee of Rama and Krishna.
They enjoyed the ghee nicely.
Such is the fate of all misers.
Their sons squander the money quickly.
Miserliness is a great curse.
The lot of misers is very miserable indeed.
They enjoy neither here nor above.
O misers! Spend your money in charity
And earn good merits now.
Charity purifies and expands the heart
And leads to God-realisation.
Do not take stale things and wear rags.
Eat well. Dress well

10. JAGULEE CHAS, BAPULEE CHAS

"Chas" in Gujrati is buttermilk.
It is "Matta" of Hindustanee.
There are three kinds of Chas, viz.,
Jugulee Chas, Bapulee Chas and Appulee Chas.
Jagulee Chas is simple very watery buttermilk.
This is given to strangers, servants and other people.
Bapulee Chas is slightly thick.
This is given to strangers, servants and other people.
Bapulee Chas is slightly thick.
This is distributed among he old father
 and sons of the family,

Friends and distant relatives.
Appulee Chas is the best buttermilk.
It is like curd and contains butter also.
This is drunk by the master of the house,
Or the proprietor, or Lala or Seth.
Similarly, man distributes watery tea,
Stale plantin, etc., to servants and others;
A little better tea and good fruits to his friends;
He takes the best tea for himself.
He closes the door when he takes the tea.
This is the play of selfishness and mean mindedness.
O Man! This will degrade you.
Give the best things to others, servants and scavenger
Treat others like yourself,
Love thy neighbour as thy self.
This will expand your heart.
And give you Immortal Bliss.

11. CRUSH THIS EGO

One teacher came to me.
He said "Mr. Ram Prasad, District Judge, Banaras,
Is my uncle's father-in-law's cousin.
Sri Biharilal, District Commissioner, Meerut,
Is my grandfather's nephew's son-in-law.
Krishna Lal, Educational Minister,
Is my father's nephew's elder brother's son.
"Achanaku Peechan Mathinike Udapranthan".
So goes the Tamil proverb.
In this world man wants to appear as a very greatman.
He connects himself with big, big officers,
They may not be his relations.
He wishes that people should take him
As a very great man and pay due respects.
This is the function of ego.
O man, such big relationship is not worth even a pie.
In what way can this help you
To attain the Supreme Peace of the Eternal?
Stand on your own leg, let your innate virtues shine.

Lead the Divine Life.
The whole world will glorify you.

12. WORLD'S TALLEST MEN

Taluks is a young man, 8ft. 3 inches tall.
Arrived recently in the village of Pegu,
Forty miles from Rangoon,
He is a native of Karena State.
He belongs to the Padaung race.
Jen van Albert, a 9 ft. 3½ in. Dutchman
Was photographed with Mr. Ramsay Maconald in 1924.
He would eat a breakfast of 3 bowls of porridge,
Four kippers, 1 lb. of fried bacon, 12 bread rolls.
And 8 cups of coffee.
Partick Colter, 8ft. 7 inches,
Used to light his pipe at street lamps.
Madhnov, a Russian, was 9 ft. 3 inches tall.
He was exhibited in London in 1905.
A tall figure is, indeed, beautiful
But too much height is ghastly and ghostly.
Maya is mysterious and unreal.
She can do anything, she can create 50 feet tall figure also.
O dwarfs! Increase your height.
Through the practise of Tadasan, etc.
Go through the article "How to grow tall"
In "The Divine Life" magazine.

13. THAT TOMORROW WILL NEVER COME

Man is ever dissatisfied.
Even if a fine meal is served,
He says "Everything was quite alright,
But there was no pickle."
Even when there is pickle
He says, "There was no *pappad.*"
He says, "I will start worship and meditation
When I become a District Judge."
When he becomes a District Judge,
He says I will start Sadhana
When I become a High Court Judge."

He says: "This time I will surely begin meditation
When my youngest son is fixed in life,
When my youngest daughter is given in marriage."
He gets double pneumonia and passes away.
He has done nothing.
O Man! Wait not for the waves to subside
To take a bath in the sea.
At once plunge; let the waves roll over you.
The mind will delude you.
Start the Sadhana now,
Whatever the circumstances may be,
And attain Self-realisation quickly.
That "tomorrow" will never come.
Many have been deceived by "tomorrow."

14. PROSPEROUS AMERICA

There are 50,40,000 families in U.S.A.
One family in two
Owns at least one acre.
One in 17 has two or more.
Seventy-seven per cent have life Policies,
With premiums of over £ 30 a year.
Forty-five per cent own
A home or a farm.
But there is spiritual bankruptcy.
They all lack in that
Supreme Spiritual Wealth.
Hence they are ever restless.
O America! Practise Tyaga,
Viveka, Vairagya, meditation,
And attain Supreme Peace of the Eternal.

15. Ph. D.

It really means Doctor of Philosophy.
People call him a doctor
Many take him to be a doctor of medicine!
Previously a doctor of medicine only was called a doctor.
Nowadays everybody is a doctor.

A D.Sc. is also a doctor.
A Chemistry Graduate is also a Ph. D.
A Botany Graduate is also a Ph. D.
This is meaningless and misleading.
This is an illusion with an illusion.
This is a delusion within a delusion.
This is Maya within Maya.
People run after these meaningless titles.
They print letter-heads with "Ph. D.
If people fail to call him "Dr. Saheb!",
He is annoyed, worried and agitated
He says: "Don't you know who I am?"
O ignorant man! Do not run after the
                        worthless shadowy toys
Do not mistake a glass piece for a diamond.
Take the essence or substance.
Mine deep and bring out the "Atmic Diamond".
Become a real Doctor of Divinity or a Sage.
And be blissful for ever.

16. MARCH OF INDIA

There is no spiritual essence in "March of India",
There is no spiritual march of India in this.
All other marches are here.
There is dancing march;
There is Bharatanatya March;
There is Billiard march;
There is horse-riding march;
There is kissing march;
There is sugar industry march;
There is a labour-welfare march;
There is military, air force, march;
There is Indian tea round the world march;
What is really wanted, what is substantial is not there.
Everything else, shadow, is there.
Man does not want higher blissful Vastu.
He runs after the shadow and perishes.

His lot is pitiable: not only this, lamentable, indeed.
O "march of India", include Sages, Philosophy, Ashramas.

17. TOPICS OF THE WORLD

Oh! What a great Joy!
Hon'ble Sri Khedkar is blessed with a son;
Maharajah Ram Singh has married Swarnalatha;
Hon'ble Andakar is now the Premier;
Oh what a great sorrow!
Mr. Robertson has divorced Elizabeth;
Bhushan Kumari was kidnapped;
Raj Kumar's only son died yesterday.
Oh! What a terrible scene!
One hundred houses were burnt last night,
Three hundred persons were stabbed,
Fifty bombs were thrown on the Station.
There was an earthquake at Lucknow,
There was cyclone at Amsterdam;
Milk is very, very dear at Badri,
Apple is very, very cheap at Srinagar.
Sambhar is nice, Rasagulla is fine,
Sweet pudding is lovely, Golkoppa is appetising.
O Man! Give up these little talks,
Talk on Brahman, the Eternal Bliss;
Soar high and attain the Infinite
Through purity and meditation.

18. THREE KINDS OF DISCIPLES

They are "Pooth", "Supooth" and "Kapooth".
Pooth is one
Who takes care of the Guru's Ashram
And nicely continues his activities.
Supooth is one
Who develops beautifully the Ashram,
Expands his work
And brings more fame to his Guru.
Kapooth is one
Who lives on what the Guru has earned,
Closes the Ashram quickly

And brings bad name to his Guru.
Vivekananda, Sradhananda, Annie Besant,
Were all Supooth disciples.
Friends! Never become a Kapooth.
Try to become at least a Pooth.

19. STORY OF A PIG

Sage Rishi Narada
Felt pity for a pig and said
"Come with me to heaven, O friend!
You will enjoy happiness for ever;
You can move in a celestial car;
You can partake of celestial feasts;
You can enjoy celestial music and dance,
Celestial damsels will serve you".
The pig replied, "O adorable Rishi!
Is there fresh offal there?"
The Rishi said, "There is no offal there".
"Then, I will not come", replied the pig!
O ignorant worldlings
Do not behave like this pig:
Do not say, "What can Moksha give me?
What is the use of entering into Nirvikalpa Samadhi?
Why lose one's own individuality?
What is the use of remaining like a
                              block of stone in Samadhi?
What power and comfort can Yoga give us?
What is the use in renouncing the world
And leading the beggarly life of a Sadhu?
O ignorant man! the pleasures of the three worlds
Are a mere drop in the ocean of bliss and Brahman.
This world is a ball of fire, is full of pains.
Know thyself and attain immortal bliss.

20. BOOT-LEGGING

Bootlegging is a variety of smuggling;
The cheat conceals opium, etc., within a special boot;
He walks decently like a gentleman.
But the expert customs officer detects him somehow

And prosecutes him.
A European lady concealed a lot of diamonds
Within the toy of her baby and escaped.
This is one form of smuggling.
Some make a hole in a book
And conceal opium in it, etc., by sticking some pages.
These also walk like gentlemen with a book in hand.
These men are also found out and punished.
Man devours diamond and gold in the mines;
He is X-rayed and given purgatives;
He too is found out!
O Man! why do you degrade yourself thus?
You are the Lord of the whole wealth of the three worlds.
Give up all these vile habits.
Meditate, realise the Lord and possess all His Wealth.

21. AN OLD LADY AND A NEEDLE

One old lady lost a needle in the house.
But she was searching for it outside
In the moon light.
One man asked her,
"O lady, what are you searching here?"
She replied, "I lost a needle in the house;
There is darkness in the house;
I am searching for it here
Because there is good moonlight here".
Worldly people are like this old lady.
They are searching for happiness in outside objects.
O man, look within; control the mind;
You will find bliss in your own Atman.

22. YOU CANNOT CHEAT THE INDWELLER

Ramakrishna was a peasant in a village near Chingelpet
He kept one hundred bags of Bengal gram in the custody
Of a petty landlord who was living near his village.
He promised to pay him a rent of Rs. 7/- monthly.
After some months the price of gram went high.
The landlord sold the hundred bags and realised a big sum.

Ramakrishna went to the landlord and said,
"How much rent should I pay? Here is the money.
Please hand over the hundred bags of gram to me now".
The landlord replied
"You did not keep with me any bag of gram.
Are you dreaming? Get away."
Ramakrishna lodged a complaint in the court.
The landlord was summoned.
He appeared in the court.
The magistrate said, "Did you get hundred bags of gram
From Ramakrishna, the peasant?
The landlord said, "Your Worship, I did not get
any bag of gram at all".
The magistrate said, "O Landlord, have pity
on the poor peasant;
Please give him back at least the empty bags.
It will be very kind of you, indeed".
The landlord thought that the magistrate was very kind.
He said, "That I can do now.
There are the hundred empty bags."
The Magistrate said to the Police Inspector,
"Arrest this man at once. He is a downright cheat."
The landlord was put in the jail for two years.
O man! do not cheat anybody.
Somehow you will be found out.
You cannot cheat the indweller.
He is ever the silent witness of your mind.

23. SUNDAY NOW FRIDAY (GANDHIDAY)

Sunday is a happy day:
Man takes rest, has no office work.
Now Friday will become a happy day:
He can play Bridge and Berique;
He can drink, smoke and gamble.
Further, he can have a decent shave.
The barber makes even an old man young!
After a shave he looks more bright;

He jumps, dances, walks with high steps;
His gait changes; he often looks at the mirror.
Too many people gather round the barber.
There is a quarrel about seniority.
Vaman applies soap himself first
In order to be the senior candidate.
But Ram who came first
Raises his first against Vaman.
One can enjoy the fun near Dharmashala.
O Man; Sunday is the best day for doing intense Sadhana.
Do more Japa, meditation and Kirtan.
Observe complete Mouna for 24 hours.
If you are earnest, if you do rigorous Sadhana,
You can realise even with 24 hours.
Waste not time in "gap", "chap",
And do not make this precious life "dawn-dhole."

CHAPTER VIII

A GUIDE TO DIVINE LIFE

1. EK NIRANJAN, DO GAD BHAD, THEEN LAT PAT

Ek Niranjan; Brahman is a spotless, secondless, one.
Whenever one is alone, he is peaceful.
Dho ghad Bhad:
In duality there are fears and quarrels.
Theen lat pat:
Whenever there are three, there are lathi charges.
Where there are three ladies, there is gun firing.
This is the reason why Lord Krishna says:
"Rahasi sthitha ekaki:
Let the Yogi constantly engage himself in Yoga
Remaining in a secret place by himself."
Narada Parivrajaka Upanishad declares:
"Wherever there are two, there is a small village;
Wherever there are three, there is a big town."
That is the reason why the girl, Dattatreya's Guru,
Broke all the bangles save one.
Even when there were two, there was much sound.
Live alone: reflect and meditate,
And attain the immortal, secondless Brahman.

2. SEE THE LORD IN ALL FORMS

Ramdas Bhadrachalam said.
"O Guru Let me have Darshan of Lord Rama."
The Guru replied
"Tomorrow the Lord will come to your house;
Get yourself ready."
Ramdas made a lot of preparation.
He made several kinds of food.
A buffalo entered the house,
Broke the pots and ate all foods.
Ramdas thrashed the buffalo.
Ramdas said to his Guru,

"I was waiting, but the Lord did not turn up."
The Guru said,
"The buffalo was no other than Lord Rama.
Lord Rama came to me and showed his back.
It was full of bruises."
Ramdas repented and cried bitterly.
Lord Rama gave him Darshan.
It is very difficult to say
In what form the Lord will appear before you.
Be on the alert.
See the Lord in all forms:
Ugly, despicable and detestable.
He may come in the form of a dog.
Leper or outcaste also.

3. THE FROG AND FAITHLESS DISCIPLES

A frog lives near the lotus;
But it does not drink the honey of the lotus.
A bee from a distant place comes
And drinks the honey of the Padma.
Some aspirants who live near the Guru
Do not imbibe the wisdom of their Guru;
They find fault with their Preceptor
And remain near him like the frog.
Some people who live in distant places
Who have intense faith in their Guru,
Who strictly follow his instructions,
Obtain the grace of the Guru
And attain the goal of life quickly.

4. BE SINCERE AND ASPIRE

Many widows visited Kamachi's Temple
In Conjeevaram in South India.
They used to pray, "O Mother, O goddess,
Give us Mukti quickly;
We are roasted in the fire of Samsara,"
They were praying for several months.
The temple priest wanted to test their devotion.
One night he stood behind the image,

He put on the golden hand of the Deity on his hand,
Moved the hand and said,
"Those who want Mukti, come to me now."
No one dared to approach the Deity.
One thought, "My grand-daughter is not married.
How can I have Mukti Now?"
Another said, "My eldest son has no children,
Let me have Mukti after some time."
Every one gave some kind of excuse.
This is the real state of affairs;
No one really wants Mukti,
It is all shallow lip-prayer and hollow devotion.

5. ASPIRE FOR LIBERATION

Once Ramprasad did severe Tapas
For a long period of twelve years.
Lord Siva appeared before Ramprasad
And said, "O devotee,
I am immensely pleased with your Tapas;
Ask a boon, I shall give you now".
Ramprasad said, "O Lord, give me a son".
Lord Siva replied, "Be it so, my child".
Ramprasad had a son,
But he was blind.
The blind son grew up into a big boy.
Ramprasad was weeping daily.
The blind son said,
"Dear father, why do you weep?"
Ramprasad replied, "Beloved child,
I did Tapas for 12 years to get a son.
I had a blind son."
The intelligent son said,
"Is there any greater blind man than you?
When Lord Siva asked you to choose a boon,
You ought to have asked him to grant Moksha."
Such is the nature of worldly people.
They do Tapas, Japa, etc., for getting worldly things.
No one cares for liberation of higher spiritual things.

6. BECOME A DOCTOR OF SOULS

One doctor says: "This is a case of appendicitis."
Another doctor says: "This is a clear case of pleurisy"
A third doctor says: "This is Hepatitis."
When doctors differ, patients die.
If the patient dies, it is cholera or pneumonia.
If the patient survives;
It is simple gastritis or simple bronchitis.
Doctor still grope in darkness.
They make experiments and kill the patients.
A doctor of soul alone is infallible
He is full of illumination and wisdom.
Therefore, become a doctor of souls.

7. PLANTS AND FLOWERS

There is the Thottavadi, "Touch-me-not", plant:
If you touch it,.it will fade.
There is the "Forget-me-not."
There is the Chinese "Forget-me-not, Cynoglossum,
Mixed and blue, which blooms on hill stations.
There is the "Lady of the Night"
That blooms and wafts fragrance at night only.
There is the "Golden Wave", Drummondie.
There are the "Morning Glories", Ipomoes.
There is the "Flowering Sage," Salvia.
There is the "Sweet William", London Tufts.
There is Haemanthus, Blood flower.
There are "Alipur Beauty", Apricot King".
There are the "Black Night",
"Yellow King Humbert", "Mrs. Lancaster".
These are all Maya's charms.
They fade away in a minute.
Delight freely in the inner eternal flower of Soul.
That fades not, that is the Beauty of beauties.
The "Soul Flower" says, "Forget-me-not",
Remember me and attain immortal bliss."

8. MILK, DOOD, PAL AND KSHEERAM

Four people were seriously fighting.
One knows English,
Another knows Hindustani,
A third knows Tamil,
The fourth knows Sanskrit.
The English knowing man wanted milk,
The Hindustani wanted Dood,
The Tamilian wanted Pal,
The Sanskrit knowing man wanted Ksheeram.
A linguist who knew all the languages
Brought each a cup of milk to drink.
They drank the milk and the fight ended.
Even so, ignorant people who do not know
The essence of all religions fight.
The essentials of all religions are the same.
Be tolerant, be catholic;
Respect all religions and all prophets;
Know the essence and enjoy the supreme peace.

9. STAGES OF MAN

The baby mews.
The child jumps, dances
And plays with toys.
The school boy walks with his books.
The grown-up boy gets degrees.
The adolescent twists his moustache,
Fights and quarrels
And runs after women;
He tries to get name and fame;
He hoards wealth;
He begets children.
Then he grows old, wears spectacles;
Puts on a dental set;
He totters with a stick;
Finally he passes away with a hiccough.
But the sage rests peacefully
In his Satchitananda Swaroopa.

10. DO NOT CHEAT

A businessman wanted to feed all the blind people.
He asked the man to beat the drum
And inform all the blind people.
All came to his house.
He asked his servants to prepare food
And all kinds of sweetmeat for one blind man.
He said to the blind men:
"It is difficult to serve item by item.
I will place the whole thing in a plate."
The blind people consented.
One plate was placed before a blind man;
Then the same plate was shifted to the second,
Then to the third, the fourth, and so on.
Lastly, that plate with food was taken away
And an empty plate was kept before each man.
Then the businessman requested the blind men to eat.
They started eating.
But there was only an empty plate!
Each blind man thought
That his neighbour had stolen the food!
They all began to fight severely.
The businessman reported the matter to the Magistrate.
The intelligent Magistrate enquired and found out
That the businessman cheated the blind people.
He put the businessman in jail for one year.
Do not cheat others.
Cheating constricts and hardens the heart;
It kills the conscience and darkens the soul;
It is a great obstacle to God-realisation.

11. ERADICATE LAZINESS

Maharaja Pratap Singh dug a pit on the road.
He put inside the pit a big golden bar.
And covered it with a big stone.
Several people were passing along the road
And cursed the man who put the big stone on the road.
No one removed the stone.

That was causing trouble to the people.
One day he asked his minister
To arrange for a meeting near the big stone.
The minister carried out the order of the Maharaja.
The Maharaja asked his servant to remove the stone.
All the people saw the big golden bar.
The Maharaja said,
"In this world all people are lazy and inert:
No one cared to remove the stone;
Everybody was cursing others.
Laziness is the cause for all deterioration.
If anyone had been energetic,
He would have obtained the golden bar."
Remove laziness, be ever vigilant and diligent.
You can attain success in every undertaking.
Yoga is not for a lazy man.

12. SEVEN AFFLICTIONS OF A PUNDIT

Ordinary people suffer from three kinds of Taapa (fire),
Viz., Adibhautik, Adidaivik and Adhyatmik.
But a Pandit suffers from four more afflictions:
They are; the misery resulting from hard study;
The misery that results from having forgotten
What was once learnt;
The misery that comes
When he is defeated by a more learned man;
And the misery that comes from pride
Or his won intellectual attainments.

13. WHO IS A SANNYASI?

A Sannyasi is one
Who has no purse of his own
But operates on the purses of all.
He has no house of his own
But lives in the bungalows of all.
He has no car of his own
But moves in the cars of all.
He is the King of kings,
without purse, treasury, car or mansion.

Glory to this King of kings.
Adorations to this Emperor of emperors.
May his blessings be upon you all.

14. WHO IS A-1 "LOOF" IN SIRSHASAN?

He is a confirmed fool
If he throws the diamond and takes a broken glass piece;
He is a first class dunce
If he throws the butter
And runs for the ghee in the market
He is A-1 'loof' in Sirshasan
If he leaves "Ananda Kutir"
And goes to the town for getting peace.
He is a capital dullard
If he leaves "Ram Nam"
Which bestows eternal bliss and immortality,
And runs after useless, earthly objects.
He is, indeed, a dull-witted one
If he leaves the company of saints and Ganga
And goes back to Bomaby again to do business
Or joins again the office with hat and boot
And signs "Your most obedient Servant"
And does Japa of "Yes, Sir. Very well Sir, Jee Hazur".
He is the most wretched man on this earth,
Shun his company at all times.

15. BEARD IS ALMOST EQUAL TO GERUA CLOTH

Some are afraid of taking Sannyasa;
Some have no qualification for embracing Sannyasa
They keep a long beard.
They apply oil and soap daily to the beard.
They comb it nicely, daily, several times.
This beard brings respect to them and food also.
Beard is their valuable property.
Ask them to remove it, they will die;
So much attachment they have to their beard.
Beard is their all in all, centre, ideal and goal.
Beard is almost equal to the orange robe of a Sannyasi.
Some fall at their feet,

Imagining they have great spiritual attainments.
In reality, they are as hollow as the bamboo.
A minutes conversation will exhibit their stupidity
And the contents of their brain.
Beware, beware of long beards.
Udaranimittam bahukrita-veshah.
Congress people are against Sannyasins
And bearded, imitation Sadhus.
Sannyasins cannot get their Bhiksha now.
Good Sannyasins will ever be honoured,
Even ministers will kiss their feet,
And fan them and drink their *charanamrit*.
Glory to Sannyasa and Sannyasins.

16. OM NAMO NARAYANAYA!

"J" said, "This is not Vedic Mantra,
This is only a Puranic Mantra."
He published an article in the Magazine.
But "R" retorted to this vehemently.
He ran to the libraries
Brought some books
And showed to "J"
That this Mantra comes in the Upanishads,
Sri Sankara has commented on this;
He also wrote in the journals.
Why this meaningless fight?
This is always the work of Pundits,
To disturb the peace of the people.
Why do you fight about "Vedic" or "Puranic?"
It is as good as 'OM' or any Mantra.
It gives Mukti or immortal bliss.
Sri Ramanuja and Prahalad and many others
Realised the glory of this great Mantra.
Waste not your time and energy in useless fights.

17. STORY OF A KING'S CAT

In days of yore there was a King.
He had a pet cat.
He used to put a lamp on its head.

He did all his work at night.
He said to his Ministers:
"O Ministers! You are not so loyal as the cat.
This cat is very sincere to me.
I place a lamp on its head
And do all my work at night."
One intelligent Minister said;
"O adorable king! I shall test this sincere cat."
He took a few rats in a small basket
And entered the King's room.
He let loose the rat in the room.
As soon as the cat saw the rats,
It jumped and seized the rats.
The lamp fell down.
The Minister said: "O King! Where is the
                                      sincerity of the cat?
There were no rats in your room
And so the cat was quiet."
The king put his head down in shame.
So long as the mind cannot get the objects,
It remains quiet for some time.
When there is the least chance.
It jumps like the cat
And indulges in sensual objects.
O aspirants! Beware, beware, beware.

18. SIVARATRI IN E.I.R.

Ramakrishna tried to enter the gate of heaven.
Indra turned him out and said,
"You are a great sinner;
You have no admission to heaven;
Go back to the world of death."
Ramakrishna said to Indra,
"O King of Paradise. I travelled in E.I.R.
In the third class, on Sivaratri
And kept vigil the whole night.
Please allow me now to enter heaven."
Indra said, "Ramakrishna, you did not keep vigil

Out of sincere devotion to Lord Siva;
There was heavy crowd, you were standing.
People pushed you hither and thither.
But anyhow you kept vigil on Sivaratri.
This is, indeed, highly meritorious.
Yes, you can enter heaven now freely."

19. STORY OF A COBRA AND A FARMER

A cobra bit the son of a farmer.
The farmer's son died.
The farmer became very angry.
He took an axe and in a hurry
Cut the tail of the cobra.
He now thought that the cobra
Would bite him in revenge.
He wanted to make peace with the cobra.
He took some milk,
And placed it near the hole of the cobra.
The cobra came and said,
"O farmer ! We cannot become friends any more.
Whenever I see you or think of you,
I will remember my cut tail.
Whenever you see me and think of me,
You will remember your dead son."
The memory of a wrong done by somebody
Is deep-rooted in the subconscious mind.
Man wants to revenge at some time.
The scar is deep and marked.
Develop intense love, forget and forgive.
Cultivate Mithya Drishti,
You can wipe out all Samskaras.

20. THE MODERN AGNIHOTRI

The other Agnihotri starts his fire in the early morning;
He offers oblation of ghee, etc.,
He propitiates the Devatas;
He purifies his heart;
He goes to Indra-loka or heaven.
The modern Agnihotri starts smoking

As soon as he wakes up.
This is the new Agnihotra.
He offers smoke oblations into his throat and nose.
He propitiates his nicotine Vasana
And the presiding Deity, "Three-Scissors,
                    Navy Cut and Three Castles".
His lips are stamped with white patches.
Any one can diagnose him as a heavy smoker.
He gets irritable tobacco heart, tobacco blindness.
He goes quickly to Yama Loka.

21. SNAKE-RAT STORY

Rats are Karma Yogins in a humourous sense,
They do not depend upon God.
They run hither and thither to obtain their food.
But (Ajagara) snakes depend upon God:
They do not move about.
If God sends some food to their abode,
They eat and remain happy.
Virakta Sannyasis do not move for their Bhiksha.
A rat saw a small bamboo basket of a snake-charmer
Which contained a snake.
It thought, "I will get good food here."
It cut the bamboo box with its teeth the whole night
And penetrated inside the box;
The hungry snake made a good meal of the rat.
Depend upon God: you will get everything.

22. GOD IS NOW HERE

Das Gupta was barrister in Patna.
He wrote on the wall of his house
"God is nowhere".
One day he argued in the court in a case.
It was a very strong case,
He had all hopes of success;
And yet he failed in his attempt.
He came to his house and was very much dejected.
His young son came to him
And read the writing on the wall

"Nowhere" was too lengthy for him.
He read it as
"God is now, here."
The mind of the barrister was entirely changed:
He became a theist.
From that day he started Japa and worship.

23. LOOK AT KALLU'S DEVOTION

Kallu was the servant of Seth Ram Das.
He used to take oath always in the name of his master,
He used to say:
"In the name of Seth Ram Das, I have told this truth".
The Seth said, "O Kallu, why do you take oath
In my name always?
In future take oath in your father's name."
Kallu replied, "O Adorable Master,
Thou art my all in all.
You give me wages, food, clothing, etc.
I depend upon you for everything.
You are really my father, protector
So I take my oath in your name."
The Seth was highly pleased with Kallu.
Even in little worldly affairs
A human being is pleased with the devotion of his servant.
Then what to speak of divine grace,
If you make total self-surrender unto the Lord?
Be devoted to the Lord: Sing His praise;
You will obtain Liberation and Immortal Bliss.

24. DO REAL SELF-SURRENDER

A half-baked devotee goes to a temple
And says, "I am Thine, All is Thine, my Lord".
As soon as he leaves the temple,
He says, "She is my daughter, he is my son".
A real, developed, devotee says
"The Lord is mine. I am His".
Then all the wealth of the Lord belongs to him.
A devotee who has made unconditional, total self-surrender

Obtains the whole wealth of the Lord
And all the wealth of this world, too.

25. DHANNA BHAKTA

He lived one hundred years ago in Punjab.
He was an agriculturist.
He was illiterate but pious, faithful and devoted.
He was simple, God-fearing and open-hearted.
On one occasion he met a saint.
The saint was worshipping a Saligram.
Dhanna said to the saint
"What are you doing, O adorable saint?"
The saint said: "I am worshipping Lord Hari in this stone."
Dhanna said, "O saint, kindly initiate me
And give me a stone for my worship".
The saint gave a big stone to Dhanna
And said, "Worship this big stone, O Dhanna".
He taught him the method of worship also.
Dhanna took the stone to his house
And worshipped it with intense devotion:
He gave up his food;
He placed some food before the stone
And said, "I will not take my food unless
 you take my offering,"
He was adamant in his resolve.
Lord Krishna came out of the stone
And took the bread and vegetable joyfully.
What is wanted is intense faith and devotion.
Such a strong faith abides in the heart
Of illiterate devotees,
But not in M.Sc's, Ph.D.s and D.Litt.s.
Glory to Dhanna Bhakta.

26. PASSION BYE-PRODUCTS

Children are the passion bye-products
Of mammy daddy
Mamma and Pappa
Amma and Appa.
The lust fire melts the butter mind,

The products are multiplying with great speed
As there is no self-restraint;
Man does not think at that moment
Whether he will be able to support them or not.
Beggars are multiplying rapidly.
It is a heinous crime
To bring forth a child,
If you cannot support and educate it
Study "Practice of Brahmacharya" and practise.
Children are sources of misery.
They bind you to the wheel of Samsara;
They intensify Moha and attachment;
They are Maya's tempting baits.
Lead a life of single blessedness
And attain the goal quickly.

27. A SADHU AND A SETH

A Sadhu went to a Seth
And asked for a ticket to Haridwar.
He did this only to test his faith.
He wanted to teach him a lesson.
The Seth said, "I will not give you a ticket,
As Sadhus sell their tickets".
The Sadhu sat in front of the Seth's house and fasted.
The friends of the Seth said, "O Seth, give him a
                               third class ticket."
The Seth agreed.
The Sadhu said, "I will accept only an Inter Class ticket now."
All the people abused the Sadhu.
They said, "Look at this Sadhu, he wants
                               an Inter class ticket!"
The Sadhu kept quiet and fasted.
The Seth's friends said "Sethji, give him an Inter class ticket!"
The Seth consented.
But the Sadhu said, "I can accept only a
                               second class ticket now."
The friends of the Seth bitterly abused the Sadhu.
The Sadhu bore the abuse patiently and fasted.

They told the Seth to give him a second class ticket.
The Seth consented.
The Sadhu said, "I can only accept a first class ticket now."
The friends of the Seth beat him severely.
The Sadhu bore it patiently and fasted.
The friends said "Sethiji, give him a first class ticket".
The Seth gave a first class ticket to the Sadhu.
The Sadhu threw it and went away quietly.
He wanted to teach the Seth
That there are very good Sadhus
Who are absolutely dispassionate.

28. CHEMO-THERAPY

Previously doctors used to raise
The power of resistance of the system
By giving tonics, etc.,
And thus eliminate the germs of diseases.
But at the present moment
Doctors practise chemo-therapy.
They give Sulphanilamides, M & B tablets,
Strong chemicals in maximum doses,
In pneumonia and other diseases.
The whole system is saturated with drugs.
All the germs die.
The patient is cured quickly.
Yoga-Vedanta Forest University, Ananda Kutir,
Also practises chemo-therapy.
Within a week—the Sadhana Week—
The worldly-minded patients are surcharged
With strong doses of Kirtan, silent, morning meditation,
Mantra-writing, lectures, Yoga Museum demonstrations,
Instructions through drama, stories, poetry, dialogues;
The germs of birth and death are destroyed.
The Sadhakas are transformed quickly.
They become Divine.

29. ANTI-PNEUMO THORAX

The surgeon makes a hole in the chest.
And draws out oxygen;

The lung collapses,
The Tubercle Baclli (T.B.) perish.
The other lung functions.
He again operates on the other side:
The collapsed lung functions now.
This is repeated alternately;
Tuberculosis is cured.
The Adhyatmic surgeon also operates:
He draws out from his patients
Vasanas, cravings and egoism.
The mind collapses (Manonash, annihilation of mind);
The germs of birth and death perish;
The patient is cured of the disease of birth and death
And attains immortal, eternal, bliss.

30. BEST LIFE INSURANCE CO.

There are many Life Insurance Companies.
There are free Insurance also.
Songsters insure their throat.
Violinists insure their fingers,
Dancers insure their feet.
But all these are worthless.
There is no safety or security.
All companies may fail.
Insure your life with God.
Do self-surrender unto Him.
Rest in Brahman or the Absolute.
You have insured everything.
You need not pay any premium.
You will attain the supreme wealth of the Lord
Plus immortality and eternal bliss.

31. ABANDON OWNERSHIP

The peasant says: "This is my land";
The Zamindar says: "No, no, it is my land";
"I have given it to the peasant for cultivation;'
The Government says, "No, no, this is a mistake:
All belong to the Government alone."
The liberated sage says

"The whole world belongs to me;
The whole world is my own Self,
The whole world is my body."
The earth is only a modification of water.
It involves itself in water.
And loses its form and says, "I am water now."
What is land? Where is land? Who is the real owner?
Think well; cogitate well.
The Lord is the real owner of this whole world.
Everything is His Maya or Lila.
Abandon possession, ownership
And possess the one Atman alone;
You are really blessed now.

32. PANDIT RAM WITH HIS THIRD WIFE

Pandit Ram Sastri is a great, learned man.
He is still living in Coimbatore;
He gives wonderful discourses,
He is a Shad-Darshan Sastri,
He knows the Gita, Upanishads, Brahmasutras, by heart.
One day he chanted Pushpanjali:
"Na karmana na prajaya dhanene
Tyage naike amritattvam anasuhu...
Not by works, not by children, not by wealth.
But by renunciation alone man attains immortality".
When he chanted this, all people laughed heartily,
Because he is not leading the actual divine life.
He has married a third wife;
He has not even a bit of renunciation;
He is clinging to his young third wife.
Mere interpretation and recitation is of no avail;
What is wanted is actual, practical, life.
Be practical and attain Self-realisation.

33. SOCRATES AND A HORSE

Somebody presented a horse to Socrates.
He said, "O Sage! This is a very good horse.
It has one hundred good qualities,
But it has one bad quality."

Socrates replied, "I can keep this horse
As it has only one bad quality
And one hundred good qualities.
May I know what is that one bad quality?"
The man replied, "the one bad quality is
That the horse is dead."
Socrates said, "I do not want this horse,
Keep it with you only."
What is life, after all, in this world?
It is mixed with death.
Attain Immortality and conquer death!
Then alone can you be very happy.

34. CHAKA CHAK

"Chaka-Chak" is something wonderful,
Laddu Chaka Chak.
"Dana-Dun" is work done continuously.
"Futa-fut" is doing a thing at once.
"Dava-dole" is to be indecisive
Or in shaky condition.
"Chatak-matak" is beauty of cloth.
Body, hairs, face, etc.
"Dil Gad gad" is joy of the heart.
How marvelous is the play of sounds!
Maya plays through sound and colours.
Don't keep your life in a Dava Dole state.
Meditate Dana Dun and Futa-fut.
Drink freely Chaka-Chak
The nectar of Immortality,
You will have Chatak-mutak face;
Your heart will be Gad-Gad.

CHAPTER IX

FALSE IMAGINATION

1. VIKALPA VRITTI

This is one of the five kinds of Vrittis
According to Patanjali Maharishi in Raja Yoga.
It does great havoc, indeed.
Vikalpa Vritti is imagination.
Maya havocs through this Vritti.
Fear, worry, co-exist with this Vritti,
There is a rumour that there is cholera
                          in George Town, Madras.
The man in Park Town falsely imagines
That he will get cholera.
He worries and actually gets cholera out of fear.
Your friend did not talk to you
As he was running in haste to catch the train.
You imagine that he was offended.
There was a rumour that a riot broke out in London.
You falsely imagine that your son,
Who was studying in London, might have died.
Eradicate these Vrittis through Vichara.
Do not identify yourself with any Vritti.
Identify yourself with the Vrittiless Brahman
And rest peacefully for ever.

2. JIVA SRISTHI ALONE GIVES PAIN

Sri Rams's son was studying in London
Sri Krishna's son was studying in Edinburgh.
A friend of Rama's and Krishna's sons
Came to India and reported to their fathers
That Rama's son was dead.
While he was actually living,
And that Krishna's son was alright,
While he was actually dead.
Rama wept bitterly and beat his breast;

Krishna rejoiced heartily.
After sometime Rama's son returned to India.
Rama's joy knew no bounds.
Krishna came to know that his son was dead.
He wept bitterly and fainted.
It is all mental creation.
Mental creation gives pain.
There is no pain in Ishvar's Srishti.
They are all aids to man.
Wind, sun, fire, etc.; give happiness to man.

3. RESTLESS HORSE-MIND

A great Badshah purchased a horse
For ten thousand rupees.
The horse was restless.
No one was able to ride on that horse
But his son Sikhandar said
"Beloved father, I can ride on this horse".
He sat on the horse.
And rode in the direction of the Sun.
The horse galloped.
The Badshah was quite astonished.
He said, "O Sikhandar! How did you manage to ride?"
Sikhandar replied, 'The Horse was afraid of his shadow.
I made the horse run towards the Sun".
Such is the restless horse mind also.
If you turn it towards Atman, it will be peaceful.
Turn it towards Maya, it will jump and dance.

4. EFFECTS OF DREAM

A king dreamt for eight hours
That he was a beggar.
Even in the waking consciousness
He felt the influence of his dream.
A beggar dreamt for eight hours
That he was a king.
Even in the waking state
He experienced the effect of his dream.
The world is a long dream or Deergha Svapna.

FALSE IMAGINATION

Wake up from this long dream;
The waking, dreaming and deep sleep states are false,
Attain the state of Turiya or the fourth,
Which is the only reality,
Which is the connecting link or witness
Of the three states of consciousness.

5. MIND IS LIKE THE FOUNTAIN PEN

A writer writes many books
With the help of the fountain pen.
The fountain pen is only an instrument of the writer,
The fountain pen should not think
"I have written all these books.
All the credit should come to me only."
Your mind, senses and the body are only instruments
In the hands of the Lord.
God does everything:
Feel like this
And abandon the doership or the agency,
You will be freed from the bonds of Karma.

CHAPTER X

VEDANTA IN HUMOUR

1. DOG IN STONE

There is a worldly proverb
"When you see a dog, there is no stone;
When you see a stone, there is no dog".
There is deep philosophy in this.
A big Maharajah had a dog
In front of his palace.
At night some officers entered the palace.
They were terribly afraid.
But the dog did not bark.
They quietly went near the dog.
They found out that it was a stone dog.
Now the dog disappeared.
It was all stone.
When there was dog, there was no stone.
When there was stone, there was no dog.
Even so, when you see the world,
There is no Brahman.
When you realise Brahman,
There is no world.

2. SUGAR CANE STORY

The farmer took bundles of sugar cans to Calcutta.
He went by train.
He thought he would get much money there.
In Howrah the ticket collector came on the train.
He said, "To whom does this bundle belong?"
The owner did not say "This belongs to me".
The ticket collector asked other co-passengers also.
No one came forward to claim the bundle.
At last one greedy Bania came forward and said,
"this is my bundle, Sir".
At once the Ticket collector said,

VEDANTA IN HUMOUR

"Pay Rs. 20/- now and take the sugar cane".
He was caught now as he had said "This is mine".
"Mamta" or mineness is the root cause of sufferings.
Remove 'I-ness' and mine-ness' you are free now.
'I-ness' comes first, then 'mine-ness' follows.

3. ATMA IS ALREADY THERE

Young Banerjee wants to possess great wealth.
He is very ambitious.
He goes to England and takes up the I.C.S. course.
He becomes a District Magistrate or a Judge.
He amasses wealth.
The young Lala or Seth desires to posses a girl,
He goes here and there and selects.
He married Usha and possesses a girl.
In these cases the objects are external to one.
But it is not the case with Atma-Sakshatkara.
Atman or the Self is already there.
It abides in the chambers of your heart.
It is your won Innermost Self.
You will have to remove the veil
And know that you are the Atman.
To know the Self is to become the Self.

4. MOORKHANANDAS

A foolish servant approached a merchant
And said: give me food only, I will work."
The merchant agreed.
He sent his servant to purchase oil.
The servant took a tumbler to the bazaar.
The bazaar man filled the tumbler with oil.
There was some balance
The servant turned the tumbler down
And asked him to fill the bottom
With the remaining oil.
As soon as the servant reached the house,
The merchant asked:
"Is this the oil you purchased?"
The servant turned the tumbler again.

Even the little oil that was at the bottom
Was spilt on the ground.
He servant said: "I had oil in the tumbler;
I turned the tumbler down
To fill the bottom with the remaining oil,
As I had no other vessel to keep it."
Virochana, the King of the Asuras, was such a fool.
He took the body as the Supreme Self.
There are many fools (moorkhanandas)
Among the Yoga-Vedanta practitioners also.

5. SLEEPWALKERS

The sleep-walker usually retains
His sense of touch but often
Temporarily loses his sense of hearing and sight.
His senses and limbs are usually controlled
By this subconscious mind to the extent
Of performing routine functions.
Sleepwalkers have been known
To saddle and ride horses
And walk many miles.
One covered seven miles.
A Californian actually swam two miles down a river
And continued his sleep upon the bank
After leaving the water.
A boy of eleven committed burglaries in his sleep.
When the police questioned the boy,
He said, "I did not do them.
But dreamt all about them".
Maya can do anything.
This is an illusory world set up by Maya.
Realise the sleepless Brahman, the Truth, and be free.

6. THE TENTH WAS MISSING

Ten persons crossed a river.
They counted their number
Just to ascertain if all of them
Had safely crossed the river.
He who counted the rest

Neglected to count himself.
They were all confirmed with the idea
That one of them was missing.
He who counted arrived at the number "nine".
He missed the fact
That the person counting was, himself the tenth person.
Each one of them, though himself the tenth,
Thought that the tenth was not there
And therefore did not exist.
The delusion is the result of ignorance.
It is known by the name "Avarana" or "Veil".
The counter concluded
That the tenth man was crowned.
He began to cry bitterly.
This also is the result of ignorance.
It is known by the name Vikshepa.

7. PROPERTIES OF THE FIVE ELEMENTS

The sound produced by air is bhuz-bhuz.
The sound produced by water is ghaz-ghaz.
The sound produced by fire is bhug-bhug.
The sound produced by earth is khat-khat.
In ether the property of sound alone is present.
In air the properties of sound and touch are present.
In fire the properties of sound, touch and form are present.
In water there are the properties of sound, touch,
form and taste.
In earth are all the five properties
Of sound, touch, form, taste and smell.
Brahman is distinct from the five elements.
The five properties of sound, etc., are absent in Brahman.
Realise this Brahman and be free.

8. VEDANTIC BOMB

A physical bomb destroys a city;
But a Vedantic bomb destroys
The city of egoism inside.
A Vedantic bomb annihilates
The illusion caused by ignorance

And makes the world vanish.
A physical bomb can destroy
Only a limited area;
But a Vedantic bomb destroys
The entire universe.
The ingredients of a Vedantic bomb
Are dispassion, discrimination,
Renunciation, aspiration.
Reflection and meditation.
Sivananda says:
Carefully mix these ingredients,
Kill the egoism by this bomb,
Enter the kingdom of Bliss
And hoist the banner of eternal Peace.

9. VEDANTIC GAZETTE, GOOD NEWS!

Hear this good news, friends,
From this Sunday supplement
Of the reputed Vedantic Gazette.
Dak Edition, from Ananda Kutir!
It will give hope to the hopeless,
Strength to the weak,
Joy to the depressed.
Your wife might have divorced you
Because you have no money now;
Your father might have left you
Because you do not earn now;
Your friends might have deserted you
Because you are in the role of unemployment;
You may be clad in rags,
You may have nothing to eat,
You may be suffering from T.B.
Leprosy and any incurable disease,
Sivananda says:
Forget the body and the Past;
You are the King of kings now;
You are the Immortal, All-blissful,
All-healthy, all-wise Soul;

You are Anamaya Atman.
Realise this birthright now
In a second, in a minute!
Feel: I am Lord of lords—
Satchitananda Svaroophoham.

10. VEDANTIC PASSPORT

You need not apply for this
To the Secretary for Foreign Affairs.
Equip yourself with the four means
Cultivate Cosmic love,
Have equal vision,
Include and embrace all,
Serve all and love all,
Feel the oneness in all,
Have adaptability, tolerance,
Patience, forbearance,
Sincerity and nobility,
Fiery spirit of selfless service
Now you will get
The Vedantic passport
In your pocket
And roam about happily
Throughout the fourteen worlds
Wherever you like.
All will recognise and welcome you,
All will adore you.
Feel: I am the all, I am all in all.
The whole world is your home—
Vasudhaiva Kutumbakam.

11. VEDANTIC SUZERAINTY

Dear Appundu!
Beloved Ammanjee!
Do not see the 'wanted' columns
Of daily papers;
Do not write in future
"Being given to understand

There is a vacancy in your office,
I beg to apply as a candidate.
As for my qualifications:
I was plucked six times
In matriculation;
I as in duty bound
Pray for your Honour's
Prosperity and posterity.....
Your obedient servant,
Appundu, Ammanjee."
Sivananda says "O Appundu!
Why do you cringe before frail man?
Kill this beggarly attitude.
Know thy essential nature:
Thou art the Emperor or emperors;
The wealth of all world belongs to you.
Feel: I am Atma Samrat,
I am above all wants."

12. ATMA BAHADURS

Old Rao Bahadurs feel miserable now
Because they have lost their titles.
But old memories bring them elation:
Just as the Bankrupt gets some pleasure
When he goes through old account books,
So also these get some pleasure
When they look at their letter-heads
And think of their past tea parties,
When people call them even now "Rao Bahadur Saheb".
Poor Rao Bahadurs! Open your eyes!
Do not be carried away by false titles
Once you were totally blind and so you were duped.
Become a real Bahadur now
By disciplining the mind and subjugating the senses
And resting in your own Satchidananda Svaroopa.
Glory to such "Atma Bahadurs"!
The Indian Union wants such Atma Bahadurs now.
May the world abound with Atma Bahadurs!

13. U. N. O.

(This Is In Lake Success, New York)

Ultimate Nameless Ocean of Bliss
Ulterior Nectarine Oasis
Ultra Nerveless One without a second
Ultra-sensual Nescienceless Overseer
Ultra-mundane Newsless Outsideless Brahman
Unadulterate Numberless Omniscience
Unaffected Noumenon Oversoul
Unalloyed Noiseless Oneness
Unattached Not-this Not-this Ocean of Joy
Unalterable Nirvana Ocean of Peace.
This wonderful U.N.O. is in countryless Niralamba Puri.
Become a member of this U.N.O. now
No fees; no degrees, but possess the four V.V.S.M.

14. SOLVE THIS RIDDLE, PLEASE

You came once
And then went away.
Then again you came
And then went away.
Now you will not come any more.
What is this?
If you cannot solve this riddle,
I shall give you the answer;
It is teeth
They came once as milk-teeth,
And then went away;
They then came as permanent teeth,
They all fall when you become old,
They will not come any more.
But Brahman never comes nor goes;
It always exists
Attain this teethless Brahman through meditation
And become Immortal!

15. SHORTAGE OF BARBERS

In Rishikesh there are 60 barbers.
But just now there are only 13.
Some have gone to attend weddings;
Some others have gone to till their lands
As this is the agricultural season.
There is scarcity of barbers now.
So some are forced to keep beards,
Some use safety razors.
Women do not bother themselves in any way
God has made them beardless.
Followers of Guru Nanak are also happy
They are not allowed to remove their hair and beard.
But there is no kind of shortage in the Eternal
There is no shortage of cloth, rice, paper,
                                              sugar or kerosene oil;
He is ever full, Paripoorna and Sampoorna;
He is beardless, hairless and bodiless.
Therefore attain Brahman and become full.

CHAPTER XI

VEDANTIC MEDICINES

1. VEDANTIC BEVERAGE

Clean your heart mortar first
With the water of celibacy.
Put some almonds of faith;
Rub them with the pestle of courage;
Add some black pepper of patience
And some Brahmic leaves of reflection,
Some cooling seeds of vigilance,
The rose petals of divine grace,
Big cardamoms of introspection,
The colouring substance of tenacity;
Now add the sugar of meditation;
Finally add the water of Immortality.
Sivananda says:
Drink this Immortal elixir, O Ram!
Madalasa gave this beverage to her children;
Sulabha drank this joyfully.
This was the favourite drink of Sadasiva Brahman,
Mansoor had this drink always in his heart theremos.

2. VEDANTIC COMPRESSED TABLET

There is the Saccharin tablet
For the diabetic patients.
There is the Amyal Nitras tablet,
For the patients of Angins Pectoris
There is the Ephaderein tablet
For the Asthmatics.
You have all sorts of tablets
For all sorts of diseases,
This is the age of tablets
Park Davis and burroughs-Welcome
Are day in and day out
Manufacturing tablets—

Yet the diseases are not cured;
New diseases are cropping up,
New 'ities', new 'orrheas'.
Sivananda says:
Use these Vedantic compressed tablets
Of Upanishadic essence;
They are the four Mahavakyas—
Prajnanam Brahma, Aham Brahma Asmi,
Tat Twam Asi, Ayam Atma Brahma.
Each Mahavakya contains
The essence of one Veda.
The whole world is compressed on OM.
All diseases will be cured,
Feel: Anamayoham—I am diseaseless Atman.

3. VEDANTIC VITAMIN

This is an age of vitamin,
The market abounds with
Vitamin A,B,C,D,E,F,G,
Allopaths do not use mixtures now;
They at once inject with vitamin A. etc.,
For any kind of disease.
This itself is a disease of the doctors.
They must be injected first with
This potent Vedantic vitamin.
This Vedantic vitamin is a cure-all;
It cures the diseases of ignorance!
It removes fear, lust, greed.
It generates knowledge.
This vitamin is Pranava or OM.
Sivananda says:
O Ram! Take this Vitamin of vitamins,
That is prepared in the laboratory of sages,
And do not take any more body.
Ask for Brahman's Brand only.
This "Vedantic Vitamin" is Brahman Itself,
The inexhaustible Source of all powers.

VEDANTIC MEDICINES

4. VEDANTIC TONIC

Discrimination	grain 20
Dispassion	grain 40
Serenity	drachm 1
Self-restraint	drachms 2
Endurance	drachms 4
Faith	scruple 1
Renunciation	minium 30
Meditation	drachm 1
Mumukshutva	ounce 1

Mix well.
Shake the bottle before use
Take one ounce twice daily.
Sivananda says:
This tonic will make you bodiless,
It will bestow immortality
Fast on Ekadasi,
Take saltless diet on Sundays,
Observe Brahmacharya,
Give up onion, garlic,
Cauliflower and turnips,
Meat, liquor and smoking.

CHAPTER XII

LESSONS FROM SCIENTIFIC INVENTIONS

1. TELEVISION

A new Television can enable you to read a book
From fifty miles away.
This is telemetering.
By this means planes will be able
To land and take off in inky darkness.
In the field of medicine, hundreds of students
Could watch an operation taking place
At a Hospital remote from the lecture room.
Develop the inner intuitive Yoga-Vision
You can have vision of the whole world;
You will experience the Cosmic Vision
Which Arjuna had through Lord Krishna's Grace.
Press the button in the Ajna Chakra,
In the space between the two eyebrows.
There flashes the Divine Light, Divya Jyoti,
That illumines the entire Universe.

2. DICTA—HELL—TELE

Dictaphone, Hell-printer, Teleprinter
Are all marvels of science.
Whatever you talk is recorded in a typewriter.
The operator should know a kind of stenography;
He reproduces the talk recorded in shorthand.
This is a great help to great writers:
They can turn out much useful work.
The Hell-printer is a cosmic instrument.
If some one types in London,
It can be recorded throughout the world;
The messages are recorded through radio waves.
Reuters have this instrument.

LESSONS FROM SCIENTIFIC INVENTIONS

Teleprinter is in use in India;
This is Hell-printer's younger brother.
All these signify oneness or unity.
They remove space or distance,
They advertise the nature of the secondless Brahman.

3. THE BIGGEST RADIO

The mind is the biggest radio;
The body is the radio-box.
Attune the mind in sweet harmony,
You can be in tune with the Infinite.
Mind is both the receiving and the transmitting instrument;
You can have television and telesound.
You can have clairaudience and clairvoyance.
You can behold distant objects and hear distant sounds.
Collect the dissipated rays of the mind,
Focus it, centre it on the Atman within,
Fix the plug of self-restraint,
Use the amplifier, "Brahmakara Vritti",
Take recourse to the "pick up" of "Vichara",
Install the loud-speaker of "Sadhana Chatushtaya",
Generate the high-volt current of intuition'.
You can hear the Anahat, the transcendental
                                        music of the soul,
The soundless, noiseless, Atmic flute.
You can realise the Immortal bliss of Brahman
Cosmic consciousness, or Nirvikalpa Samadhi.

4. REMOVE THE DIRT IN THE MIND-RADIO

A new Radio is fixed.
All its parts are quite alright.
But the message is not received.
This is due to a particle of dirt in it.
If the dirt is removed,
All the messages and songs will be heard distinctly.
Even so, on the big radio of the mind.
If there is dirt or bad character or evil quality,

It cannot express true joy, bliss, love,
The spirit of self-sacrifice, the aroma of truth.
Remove the dirt of evil traits.
Fill the mind with divine virtues;
You will shine with Brahmic aura.
You will shed the light of Self-illumination.

CHAPTER XIII

HUMOUROUS PIECES

1. EAR COMPLAINS TO THE LORD

O Lord! You have been partial.
You gave the mouth good protection;
It can shut itself
And remain quite peaceful.
The eyes also can do the same;
The eyelids close and protect them;
They can no longer see objects,
They can also remain very peaceful.
But nothing can shut myself.
All sorts of sounds pour into me;
I am very much disturbed.
The Lord replied, "I am not partial
I will sit myself at your door
And save you from disturbing sounds.
Wear a small Rudraksha earring;
I will dwell there as your servant.
Practise Pratyahara or abstraction.

2. TO LORD KRISHNA

O Lord Krishna, Joy of Devaki,
Please do not come to Brij now.
You will experience great difficulty.
You cannot get butter and curd now.
There is rationing everywhere.
You will get a ration card,
Only for six Chhataks of Atta-chawal.
You will have to appear in rags;
You cannot wear silk Pitambar.
Please remember this point well.
Further, you will have to stand and stand for hours together
And march slowly in "queues" order;
You will lose your patience.

This is the miserable state of affairs now.
People hope to see better days
From the "Grow more food Campaign."
God only knows what will happen.

3. HOW TO BECOME A FAMOUS SADHU

It is very easy for a Sadhu to become very famous;
Keep a long beard and observe Mouna;
Stand up on one leg for two hours;
Walk naked;
Live in a cave for two months;
Eat nim leaves or drink cows urine;
Wear a Gunny bag;
Have good, long, matted-locks;
Sit on a pose for one or two hours;
Keep a Hamsa-danda or Yoga-danda;
Deliver some Gita or Vedantic lectures;
Talk anything nonsensical or irrelevant;
Cut the frenum of the tongue,
And take water through the nose or anus;
Advertise falsely "I have many great Yogic Powers."
Common people look to external marks or signs.
It does not matter where and how the mind of the Sadhus is.
Now you can build kutirs easily.
Now you can have easily many disciples,
Now you can add 108 Sri, Yogiraj or
                        Parivrajak Paramahamsa,
You will have a large following.
You can cheat any number of people in any way.

4. TAMARIND BRAIN

Madrasees have "Tamarind brains".
Tamarind brains work wonders.
Ramanujam (Mathematician) had a tamarind brain.
Sri Sankaracharya and Ramanuja had tamarind brains.
Subramania Bharathiar also is a tramarind brain.
There is a special mysterious Vitamin in tamarind.
It is "Brain Vitamin X Y Z",
It is also known as "Tamiro-Vigorine".

It energises the Pineal and Pituitary glands.
It beautifully sharpens the intellect,
Excels Lecithin, phosphorous and yolk of eggs,
Gives vigour to the brain cells,
Bestows acumen, wisdom, discrimination,
And makes one a genius or prodigy.
Glory to Tamarind and "Tamarind Brains".

5. MIXED ACTION

Actions are of three kinds
Viz., good, bad and mixed.
Good Karmas make you a God in heaven;
Bad Karmas throw you in lower wombs;
Mixed actions give you a human birth.
If you rob a man and feed the poor,
It is a mixed action.
If you earn money by unlawful means
And build a temple or hospital,
This is a mixed action.
If you get money by cheating a man
And construct an Ashram for Sannyasins,
This is also a mixed action.

6. ANT, LIKE THE ATOM BOMB

The ants are very small or tiny;
But they can do superhuman feats:
They can carry a serpent even.
The red ants can give a very sharp sting.
They enter the nose of big elephants,
Agitate and make them run hither and thither.
A small ant enters your ears at night
And teases you to an enormous degree.
A Large army of ants attack you at night
And disturb your sleep.
Keep any box with sweetmeats anywhere,
They will penetrate and taste them first.
You cannot separate sugar when it is mixed with sand;
But they can separate the sugar very easily.

7. ELECTION AND VOTING

Cars run hither and thither with flags and boards.
"Vote for Mr. "So-and-so", "Vote for Ram Prasad."
Tea hotels and sweetmeat shops are fully crowded.
There are ringing of bells and "Jeya-Jeya-kar".
Boys dance in ecstasy after chota-hazri.
There is much Tamasha, fun and amusement.
Some spend thousands and lacs of rupees,
To get success and name.
Some weep, repent and die when they fail:
Some voters are confused when they see
                              red, green, white boxes.
And put their slips in wrong boxes.
There is fighting, stabbing and shooting in Poling Stations
A very long list of electoral roll is prepared.
Some are dead, some are absent.
Voters go in decent cars.
But they return walking; no one cares for them now.
Democracy is good; adult Franchise is good;
But there should be quality in the voters.
The voters should be cultured, conscientious and pious
Then alone will the result be satisfactory.

8. TWINS AND TRIPLETS

Twins occur once in 85.2 cases,
Triplets occur once in 7628.7 cases,
Quadruplets occur once in 6,79,734 cases.
A Russian peasant, Wasilef, married twice.
He had 87 children by his two wives.
The first wife had four quadruplets,
Seven triplets and sixteen sets of twins;
The second wife had triplets twice
And twins six times.
A Negress in the Gold Coast
Had in 1903 sixtuplets:
Five boys and one girl.
An Italian woman gave birth to 20 sons:
First confine nine; second time eleven.

The marriage of twins increase the likelihood to twins
A woman doctor, Mary Austin,
Had 13 sets of twins and six sets of triplets:
A total of 44 children.
If we have some more Wasilefs and Mary Austins,
We want some more physical universes.
The Census Reporters will surely be quite tired;
Ration Officers and Inspectors will run away.
We want twin, triplet and quadruplet Sages:
Two, three or four Sages in each district.
Then the world will be a supreme Paradise.

9. GLORY TO NEWSPAPER BOYS

Thomas E. Dewey,
Governor of New York
And candidate for Presidentship in 1944 and 1948,
Started his career as a newspaper boy.
General D. Eisenhower,
The hero of World war II,
Was also a newspaper boy.
Benjamin Franklin, Henry Ford,
Pioneer of the automobile industry,
Thomas A. Edison,
Who developed the electric light,
Herbert Hoover, former President of the United States,
Were all newspaper boys.
Newspaper Boy Day also is observed in U.S.A.

10. PROCREATE LESS' CAMPAIGN

The Government of India have started
"Grow more food campaign."
This is extremely good.
We will soon have plenty of grains, etc.
Even H.E. Sri C.R. is at the plough.
Side by side we should have
"Produce less children campaign".
This is a complementary or supplementary campaign.
Children beget children

And bring forth more beggars in this land.
They can neither feed, nor clothe, nor educate them.
Diplorable, ignominous, depreciable, state of affairs!!
This should be done,
Not through Malthusian appliances or French Letters—
This will prove, indeed, a thorough failure—
Not through legislation or bills,
But through the practice of self-restraint or Brahmacharya,
Through proper understanding and knowledge.
The brutal pig element should be annihilated
Through prayers, Japa, enquiry and meditation.
Then there will be no annual crop of children.
If any one fails to observe self-restraint,
Then show a black flag to him,
When he moves about with a battalion of beggars,
And make him come to his senses.

11. HUSBAND AND WIFE

Lightning is the wife of cloud.
Sperm is the husband of ovum.
Power is the wife of a politician.
Santi is the wife of a Sage.
Samadhi is the wife of a Raja Yogi.
Faith is the wife of a devotee.
Sacrifice is the wife of a Karma Yogi.
Japa is the wife of a Mantra Yogi.
Anahat is the wife of a Laya Yogi.
Siddhi is the wife of a Kundalini Yogi.

12. THREE INCHES INTELLECT

Many have a 3 inches intellect.
What is this 3 inches intellect?
Man is swayed by 3 inches tongue,
He lives to please this 3 inches tongue;
Such a man has a 3 inches intellect.
There is nothing for him beyond eating.
There is nothing for him beyond sense-pleasure.

Others have five feet intellect:
They think of this body alone,
It comforts, needs and other things.
They live for attaining these objects.
Some others think of three lives
Past, present and future;
Discrimination has just dawned in them.
Some think of the one, pure, Atman,
What is beyond the three Gunas and senses.
There are the wisest among men.

CHAPTER XIV

SIVA'S NATIVE PLACE

1. GOODBYE, VAIN WORLD

Goodbye, vain world, I am going home,
My original, sweet abode of Immortal Bliss.
Thou art the product of Maya.
There is nothing in you.
You are full of pains, sorrows and temptations;
And yet you attracted me much.
I roamed here and there in vain.
But now I have found out thy tricks.
I am Brahman, thy source and womb.
Goodbye, false world, I am going Home.

2. SONG OF VIBHUTI YOGA

(Thars: Sunaja)

Bhajo Radhe Krishna
Bhajo Radhe Shyama........
I am spinach among leafy vegetables;
I am almond among all nuts;
Milk am I among perfect foods;
Tomatoe am I among all vegetables;
I am potato among tuber and roots;
I am Basumati rice among all cereals;
Soya bean am I among all pulses;
Cow's ghee am I among all fats;
I am mango among all kinds of fruits,
I am "Alphonso" among all mangoes;
Buttermilk am I among all beverages;
Glucose am I among all sugars;
I am phosphorus among all minerals;
I am vitamin C among all vitamins;
Lady's finger am I among green vegetables;
Barley water am I among invalid foods;

I am first class Protein in milk among all proteins;
I am white sugar among carbohydrates;
Turnip am I among English vegetables;
Lemon juice am I among anti-scorbutics.

3. MY NATIVE PLACE

In my native place there is a mystic river
Whose water is honey, milk and nectar,
He who drinks it, becomes Immortal.
In my native place there is an Immortal tree
Whose fruits bestow deathlessness.
In my native place there is neither day nor night
But there is always eternal sunshine.
In my native place there is neither pain nor grief,
Neither hunger nor thirst, neither disease nor death.
But there is ever peace, bliss and joy.
In my native place there are neither thieves nor dacoits,
Neither Municipality nor notified area,
Neither Legislative Assembly nor Privy Council.
My native place is Brahma Puri,
Near Ananda Kutir, on the bank of Jnana Ganga,
In the illimitable domain of Niralambapuri.
Maya dares not enter here.
There is the invulnerable fortress of Vairagya
Come, come, my friends! live here. Be quick!
Tarry not, delay not; enjoy the wisdom bliss.
Cordial greetings! Welcome beloved comrades!

4. THE COW TREE!

There is a tree in Venezuela
Which gives pure "cow's" milk.
You have only to make a hole in it;
Pure milk issues forth from it.
India also will have such trees shortly.
May India abound in "Cow trees"!
Then there will be no milk shortage.
All people will be healthy and robust.
Food problem also will be solved.
In India, in the Himalayas,

There are several "cow-trees", Kamadhenus,
You have only to approach them with bhava;
And, they will give you an abundance of
The milk of Eternal Wisdom.
These trees are the Sages of Intuitive Wisdom
And Self-realisation.
Serve them, prostrate to them and ask them:
They will feed you with the milk of wisdom.
The west needs the seeds of this Kamadhenu.
The East should spread their teachings
And produce these Wisdom-trees in the West, too.
Then there will be Peace and Happiness
Throughout the world.

5. INTOXIMETER AND MAYAMETER

This tests the degree of drunkenness.
The drunkard blows a balloon.
The air in the balloon then bubbles
Through a tube filled with purple liquid.
If the liquid loses its colour in 90 seconds,
There must be enough alcohol
In the drunkard, to influence his judgment.
That is the first stage—"delighted and devilish"
The other three stages are—
"Dizzy and delirious";
Dazed and dejected and "dead drunk".
"Walking the chalk-line "and "tongue twisting"
Are other tests in Scotland Yard.
A few sips may not impair a driver's
Ability to handle the controls quickly;
But they always influence his judgment,
Leading a driver to take risks
He would normally avoid,
And are a far commoner cause
O road accidents than clumsiness.
The other spiritual "Intoximeter"
Detects the degree of Moha or pride
Due to learning, possessions, Siddhis, position, etc.

It is Maya-meter.
It is more sensitive than the other one.
It is used in the Ananda Kutir Laboratory.

6. SONG OF HONEY

Ananda Thene	Brahmananda Thene
Thene Thene	Thene Thene
Thene Thene[1]	Thene Madhuve
Thene Thene	Thene Honey-ye
Celestial Thene	Divya Madhuve
Ananda Thene	Brahmananda Thene
Adwaita Thene	Anubhava Thene
Chidghana Thene	Chinmaya Thene
Chinmaya Thene	Chinmatra Thene
Nirakara Thene	Nirguna Thene
Niramaya Thene	Nirvisesha Thene
Nitya Mukta Thene	Nitya Suddha Thene
Nitya Siddha Thene	Nitya Buddha thene
Nityananda Thene	Paramananda Thene
Sankara Anubhava Thene	Datta Anubhava Thene
Soham Thene	Sivoham Thene
Sivoham Thene	Soham Soham thene
Soham Soham Thene	Svaroopoham Thene
Ananda Thene	Brahmananda Thene

7. 'DIGAMBARA' SONG

Digambara Jaya Digambara Digambara Jaya Digambara
Digambara Jaya Digambara Sripadavallabha Digambara
Atri Nandana Digambara Anusuya Putra Digambara
Antarai:—Digambara Digambara Digambara Digambara

8. RAM KIRTAN

Bhajo Ram Bhajo Ram Bhajo Ram Bhajo Ram
Bajo Ram Bhajo Ram Bhajo Ram Bhajo Ram
Chupuke Chupuke Dheere Dheere
Ankomse Manme Anevale

---

1 Note: Thene in Tamil means "O Honey!"

Secretly secretly quietly quietly
Through the eyes into heart anavale.

9. THAT DIVINE WHISKY

O Man! Drink that wine which is nectar of Immortality,
Drink that cock-tail which gives you God-intoxication,
Drink that Punch which opens the eye of intuition
Drink that brandy which is the foundation of joy and bliss
Drink that liquor which bestows you eternal life.
Drink that Vermouth which will give you Samadhi.
Drink that portwine which cures birth and death
Drink that Johny Walker born in 1838 (Anadikal)
          which gives you super-consciousness,
Drink that ale which will give you cosmic vision
Drink that squash which will give you cosmic consciousness.
Drink that beer which will make you sing Hari OM
Drink that Exshaw which will make you dance
          in divine ecstasy.
That Divine Whisky is Japa, Kirtan, meditation
          and enquiry of who am I?

10. NATURE CURIST IS INTOLERANT

A Nature curist is terribly intolerant.
His target is always an allopath or allopathy.
If he writes a book,
He writes very little on Nature Cure
But his criticism on Allopathy
Covers hundred pages.
Clairvoyantly you can see in his brain darting red arrow.
He keeps a little friendship with Homeopathy.
Glorify your own system;
But why do you vilify other systems?
God is Infinite.
Nature of man is diverse.
Therefore, different systems are needed.
Each system exists
Because there is some truth of good in each system.
Each system suits a particular nature.
Therefore, behold good or God in each system.

Quarrel not, become wise.
Slay this intolerance, the enemy of wisdom and peace.

11. NATURE CURIST VRITTIS

A Nature Curist has sometimes enema-Akara Vritti
He thinks of enema very often.
He has at other times fasting-Akara Vritti;
He speaks of fasting and fasting alone.
He has sometimes mud-plaster-akara Vritti.
He thinks of mud cure or earth-cure
He has sometimes vegetable-soup fruit juice Akara Vritti.
He talks of vegetable soup and fruits juice only.
He has sometimes hip-bath-akara Vritti;
He speaks of hip-bath, spinal bath and sitz bath,
The mind assumes forms of what one thinks.
Even in dream he gives enema and hip-bath.
Such is the force of waking state thoughts.
Where is the place for Brahmakara vritti?

12. ALLOPATHIC MONSTERS

The monsters of the Puranas
Have not done so much havoc
As the allopathic doctors
By their drugging and drugging the patients
They have killed millions.
For each patient
They must give at least
Two kinds of tablets, three kinds of powders.
One ointment, four kinds of mixtures.
Five kinds of tonics, and
Three kinds of injections—
A powder at bedtime!
A cathartic tablet at 8 p.m.
Every pore should emit some sulphanomide smell.
Then alone are they satisfied.
The bill should come to at least Rs. 25/- a day.
This has become their habit,
A terrible, inveterate disease.
O Man! Take recourse to Nature Cure

And thus save doctor's bills;
Qualify yourself as your own doctor.

13. NATUROPATH'S POOR PRARABDHA

A Naturopath ought to have been
A big miser in his previous birth
He might have not performed
Any charitable act in his last birth.
He might not have fed even a single man.
In this birth or Janma.
So he lives on one meal,
Half a meal, or one and a half meal;
Some cocoanut, some nuts, some roots;
Some days he goes without food,
This is nature's punishment.
This is the inexorable law of cause and effect.

14. THE FAMILY OF EGOISM

Egoism is the householder
Mind is his wife.
Prana is his servant.
Senses are his children.
Body is his house.
Soul is the light of the house.
Causal body is the cot or bed-stead.
Desire is the fuel.
Thought is the fire.

15. THE BEST—I

God is the best Doctor.
Mother Nature is the best physician.
Ganga water is the best drink.
Pranayama is the best exercise.
Brahmacharya is the best tonic.
Mango is the best fruit.
Spinach and Parwal are the best vegetables.
Buttermilk is the best drink for health.
Fasting is the best medicine.
Meditation is the best divine elixir.

Nature-cure is the best cure.
Raw vegetable food is the best food.

THE BEST—II

Tea: says the Gujarati.
Coffee: says the Madrasi,
Rasagulla: says the Bengali,
Pooranboli: says the Maharatta,
Peda Lassi: says the Punjabi,
Food says the glutton,
Money: says the miser,
Health: says the doctor,
Power: says the politician,
Beauty: says the artist,
Music: says the songster,
Love: says the damsel,
Liquor: says the drunkard,
Selfless service: says the Karma Yogi,
Bhava Samadhi: says the Bhakta,
Asampranjata Samadhi: says the Raja Yogi,
Brahma Jnana: says the sage.

16. LECTURE BY MILK

Ladies and Gentlemen!
I am the perfect food among all foods.
I contain highclass proteins and vitamins.
I impart good health, vim and vigour.
I am the food of Rishis, Sages and Saints.
I am the food of children, invalids and convalescents.
I contain within myself butter, cheese and cream.
I build your bones and flesh.
I make your body grow.
Without me tea and coffee are useless.
I am in the form of **kheer, peda** and **kalakand,**
Condensed milk, Horlicks, Mellins are my forms.
People are dying for me in the morning.
This world is a void minus me.
Take care of the cows, I shall take care of you!

17. SONG OF ASANAS

(One morning Sri Swami Sivanandaji thought: 'We must adopt the very methods which the materialists adopt to win man over to their side, in order to counteract their propaganda and to wean man away and lead him Godwards.' In order to popularise the practice of Yoga Asanas, Siva composed the following songs. You can sing this in the same tune as the street sweetmeat hawker's:-

Pisa Pisa Mittai Hai
Garam Garam Mittai Hai
Thaja Thaja Mittai Hai

Sri Swamiji has also composed another song "the Song of Govinda" in the same tune and has put into it many invaluable lessons on Yoga and Sadhana.

During his recent All-India Tour, Sri Swamiji sang the following Asana-Song at several centres and the audience liked it immensely.)

Padmasan is	Lotus Pose.
It is ideal for	meditation
Gheranda, Sandilya	liked it much.
Ladies can sit in	Padmasan.
Sidhasana is the	Perfect Pose.
Excellent for	Brahmacharya.
Countless Siddhas	Practised this.
Practitioner gets	many Siddhis.
Hence the name	Siddhasan.
King of Asanas	Sirsasan.
Jawahar roj	Kartha hai
Even now	Kartha hai
Stalin also	Kartha hai
Churchill also	Kiya hai
Gandhi liked it	very much.

SIVA'S NATIVE PLACE

Rajen Babu . . . . Is doing it.
Memory power . . . . develops much
This is good for . . . . Brahmacharya.
Health and long life . . . . paathaa hai

Oordhvareta . . . . Hota hai
Moksha dene . . . . vala hai

Sarvangasan is . . . . equally good.
Thyroid gland is . . . . exercised.
Long life dene . . . . vala hai
Old age door ho . . . . jayega.
Always youthful . . . . you will be.
Brahmacharya-ko . . . . Achcha hai
Kundalini is . . . . awakened.

It is cure for . . . . all diseases
Halasan is good . . . . along with this.
Matsyasan is the . . . . fish pose.
This is done after . . . . Sarvangasan.
Lungs are greatly . . . . expanded.
It helps deep— . . . . breathing.
It removes . . . . constipation.

Paschimottanasan . . . . Bahut Achcha hai
Gastric fire paida . . . . kartha hai.
Constipation cure . . . . kartha hai.
Piles diabetes . . . . jatha hai.
This cures lumbago and . . . . myalgia.

Mayurasan is . . . . Peacock pose.
It is a beautiful . . . . Asan hai.

Wonderful Asan hai	for digestion.
Liver achcha kam	karta hai.
It awakens the	Kundalini.
Ardha Mastsyendrasan	Twists the spine.
Appetite is greatly	increased.
Abdomen is	massaged.
Back muscles are	exercised.
Bhujangasan is the	Cobra Pose.
Ye spinal column-ko	achcha hai.
Abdomen is greatly	strengthened.
This is an all-round	Exercise.
Dhanurasan is a	Combination.
All the muscles are	exercised,
More vigorously than	Bhujang Salab.
Padahasthasan wonderful	Asan hai.
Vertical Paschimottan	Asan hai.
Flatulence-ko	bahuth Achcha hai.
Trikonasan is a	good twist.
Hip muscles are	exercised.
Ey bhi bahuth	Achcha hai.
Uddiyana Nauli	Roz karo
You will get good	digestion.
Kundalini will be	awakened.
Health and long life	you will get.
Bhukthi Mukthi	you will get.
Chiranjeevi	you will be.

Savasan do at the	end of all.
You will have	peace and rest.
These are all	Divine Mittai.
Matsyendranath	Ate these.
Siva also	Bahut Khaya hai.
Yogis Siddhas	Khaya hai.
Jivanmuktas	Khaya hai.
Therefore thum bhi	Khavo
Bhukti Mukti	Pavo.

(You, too, can sing this song and inspire your friends and children. Specially the youngsters will like it very much. The mixture of English and Hindi will amuse them and will enable them to grasp the ideas quickly and well.)

18. INCOMPATIBLES

This world is full of incompatibles
Alkali and acid are incompatibles.
Potassium iodide and Spirit etheris nitroci are incompatibles.
Homeopathy and Allopathy are incompatibles.
A hot wife and calm husband are incompatibles.
A religious husband and an irreligious
                                      wife are marked incompatibles.
Mr. Banerjee and Mrs. Boots Bannerjee are incompatibles.
A pure mind and an impure mind are incompatibles.
An aspirant and a worldly-minded man are incompatibles
Atman and sensual objects are incompatibles
Maya and Brahman are incompatibles.
Vidya and Avidya are incompatibles.

Section II

PHILOSOPHY IN HUMOUR

1. TO LORD KRISHNA

O Lord! Beloved of Radha,
Now do not come to Brij,
You will find entire change.
You will be quite amazed.

The pastures where cows were grazing,
Are all cinema halls,
Hotels clubs, restaurants,
And modern new theatres.

When you were in Muttra
All people had rosaries in their necks,
Now they put on ties and bows
And thick double collars.
They were drinking Yamuna water,
Now they drink soda, lemonade,
Sometimes "drinks"
"Born in 1850, still go strong".
They were wearing head turbans
And saluting "Jey Sri Krishna"
Now all wear hats and boots
And say "Good morning" Good night, Sir".
"Adabars Janab",
Rai Sahibji, Salam.

2. MAYA

Maya is not that'
It is not Brahman
It is the illusory power of God
It is neither Sat nor Asat.
It is *Anirvachania*

You can not describe It;
It is the inscrutable Sakti,
That deludes people.

You know there is no pleasure
In all worldly objects
Yet you cling to them:
This is Maya.

You know you will die,
Yet you think,
'I will live for ever;
This is Maya.

You make a firm resolve
When you are in the burial ground
'I will lead a virtuous life'
'I will worship God'
You forget it as soon as you reach home
This is Maya.

You know it is wrong
To tell lie, to be selfish
Yet you speak lies, you are selfish,
This is Maya.

Whenever you are in distress,
You think of renouncing the world,
As soon as the trouble is over,
This world is all joy for you.
This is Maya.

Whenever your wife quarrels,
You think of abandoning her;
She again smiles,

You cling to her like a leech,
This is Maya.

You know that this body is impure and inert,
Yet you adorn it, worship it,
You take it as the pure Self.
This is Maya.

Woman is *Chaitanya Maya,*
Money is *Jada Maya;*
These are her two baits,
To entrap the poor Jivas.
Renounce lust and money,
There is no world for you,
You will conquer Maya,
You will attain Immortality.

Mysterious is this world of the mind,
More mysterious is Maya
Still more mysterious is Brahman,
To know Him is to conquer Maya.

3. DAYA KRISHNA AND DAANAVEER RAM

There is a big officer in Calcutta,
His Name is Daya Krishna;
But really he has a stony,
Sin-hardened, barren heart.
He takes bribes and teases the inferiors.
He is a burden on the earth.
O God! Punish this man severely!
Correct and mould him,
Make him a real merciful man.

There is a big merchant in Bombay
His name is Daanaveer Ram
But he is a first class miser,
He never spends a pie in charity,

He hoards and hoards wealth.
He counts and counts his wealth day and night,
He sleeps by the side of the iron safe,
He eats stale vegetables,
He ties the keys in his sacred thread
O Lord! teach this man a lesson,
What is the use of his living in this earth?
Melt his stony heart,
Make him a charitable man.

There is a Doctor in Delhi,
His name is Khusdil Ram,
He has plenty of property,
But he always worries himself,
For money and money alone,
He charges even when the patient dies,
He sends a stiff bill,
Even to his father and brothers.
He is ever restless,
He counts his daily visits.
This is his daily worship,
This is his daily spiritual diary.
Mercy and sympathy are unknown to him.
Can he dream of salvation, O Lord?
Is there any way out for him?
He is committing horrible sins daily.

Pray O Lord be merciful to this wretch also!
He does not know what he is doing,
He is also Thy creation,
But a wicked arrogant child.

There is a big Engineer in Lahore,
His name is Pavitra Ram.
But purity is unknown to him,
He drinks heavily at the club.
He eats meat, fish and garlic.

He earns money by hook or crook.
He visits unholy places.
He makes false bills.
Honesty is unknown to him.
He concocts, cooks, connives.
O Lord! Holy of holies!
Make him a real Pavitra Ram.
Obstruct him, save him,
Employ him, guide him,
Still there is hope for him.

4. "TOR" KA "DUR"

The sound 'tor' causes 'dur',
The ending 'Tor'
In Collector, Doctor
Causes 'Dur' or fear
In the clerks and the sick.
The compunder has *dur* for the Doctor.
The Tahsildar has *dur* for the collector.
The motor driver has *dur* for the cylinder,
For it may stop at any time.
The Secretary has *dur* for the Minister.
The Minister has *dur* for the Prime Minister.
He who travels without ticket.
Has *dur* for the ticket collector.

Be afraid of sin.
But fear in the Lord
Is the beginning of wisdom.
Give up *Torka dur*,
Attain the fearless Brahman,
And rest in Supreme Peace.
'Dur' literally means fear. The sound 'tor' causes fear (dur).

5. STORY OF ADE VADA

In the soundless, noiseless Brahman or the Eternal who is silence and peace itself, a vibration (spandan) arose through his Sankalpa. Brahman wanted to become many:

"Ekoham Bahu Syam." Before the creation the three Gunas were in a state of equilibrium, or poise (gunasamyavastha). When there was vibration, creation started. The three Gunas *sattwa, rajas* and *tamas* manifested themselves. When there was vibration, a primordial sound arose. That sound was OM or Pranava. From OM emanated all sounds words, languages, names and forms, and worlds.

Name and form are inseparable. Thought and words are inseparable. Brahman and Maya are inseparable. *Sakta* and *Sakti* are inseparable. Every sound produces an image. A sound that is uttered is never lost. It is recorded in the *Akasa*. Sound is the quality of *Akasa tattva* and is transmitted through air.

This world is mere sound. Imagine for a moment that there is no sound in the world. The world vanishes. It is the sound that first put the mind in motion, that first made the mind think. Vedas are sounds. Vedas are *Sabda Brahman.*

A sound has Artha or meaning. It gives knowledge or Jnana. Sabda, Artha, and Jnana go together. You hear the word 'cow'. It is a sound. It gives you meaning and knowledge. During meditation also the mind will be thinking of the words and their meanings, through the force of habit. It will bring out the words from the bed of Samskaras in the subconscious mind or *chitta*.

There are two *vrittis* in a sound, viz, *sakti vritti* and *lakshana vritti*. *Sakti vritti* gives power to the sound. *Lakshana vritti* generates meaning.

If you praise a man and say "He is a very good songster"; the songster is immensely pleased. There is power in the word, "good". If you say to a man "You are a rogue," he will kick you. There is power in the word "rogue". "Sala" means in Hindi "brother-in-law". If you say to a man in anger "Sala" he will beat you. Mark how a word, agitates the mind of a man. One word gives pleasure and elevates the mind. Another word gives pain and perturbs the mind. This is due to the *sakti vritti* of the words. Maya operates through words. She does *sabda jalam*. She plays through the jugglery of words.

Now I come to the story of 'Ade-Vada". "Ade" means in Tamil "tu"—"you". "Va" means "come". The elder brother says to his younger brother "ade vada" "come here". The master says to his servant "ade vada". There is lack of respect when you say "ade vada". "Varungal" is a respectful term. There is courtesy also. It means, "Venerable, sir, kindly come". If you say *"ade vada"* to a respectable person, he will be at once greatly annoyed. He will become infuriated and give you blows also.

A sage is not affected by the play of words. He is the same in praise or censure. He knows that words or sounds are mere vibrations in the air. Only a weak, worldly-minded man is seriously upset by words. Whenever anybody abuses you, stand adamant. Reflect and enquire. Rise above jugglery of words. Do not pay any attention. Say unto the mind. "O mind! Do not be agitated. It is only a mere sound. The abuser is only wasting his energy and spoiling his tongue." Gradually you will gain strength. You will not be moved by ridicule, abuse, censure, criticism, etc.

You must develop austerity of speech. Whatever you speak, must be truthful and beneficial. Your speech must not give annoyance to anybody. You must not use any abusive words. You must not say "ade vada". You must address everybody "Maharaj", "Bhagavan", "Narayan", "Varungal", "ayiye", "Ji". This needs discipline of speech, and control of impulses. If you use respectful terms that shows you possess refined, noble character and very good manners.

Even a highly educated man carried away by the impulse of speech when he is angry. He speaks anything. He utters all sorts of abuses and repents when he comes to normal state.

Ordinarily, a worldly man by nature treats others with contempt. He will not respect others. He cannot use respectful terms. He will never say "Ap, Maharaj". He wants that others should respect him and address him with dignified terms and titles. If you once fail to use title "Rai Saheb" to a man during conversation or in business letters, he is annoyed. How silly and degraded man has become! Slave of words, slave of titles, slave of respect and honour, slave of woman, slave to tongue, slave of tea, slave of senses! Pitiable is his lot! Thousand times deplorable is his plight ! And yet he boasts of his intellect, position, rank, titles and attainments. O little ignorant man! Rise above all these. Give up artificial living. Regain your lost divinity. It is not too late even now.

May you all develop refined manners and respect others with Narayana Bhava! May you all attain high culture and speak sweet words—truthful, elevating and inspiring words! May you all attain the highest state of supreme, stupendous, silence or Maha Mouna where there is neither noise nor sound!

6. SPRITUAL SMOKING

Spiritual smoking is inhalation or absorption of the idea "I am Brahman—I am the immortal Self" and giving out the smoke of "I am not this perishable body." Spiritual smoking is absorbing of the divine virtues viz, forgiveness, mercy, pure love, truthfulness etc., and giving out the smoke of hatred, lust, greed etc. Sri Sankara and Dattatreya, Madalasa and Sulabha, Mansoor and Shams Tabriez practiced this sort of smoking throughout the twentyfour hours and enjoyed the eternal, unparalleled bliss. They did not suffer from nicotine poisoning, tobacco heart and tobacco Amblyopia.

In a moment the cigar or cigarette or the Beedi is reduced to ashes. This reminds you of the perishable nature of this body and all objects of this world. This body is cremated. The ash is left behind. And yet you repeat again and again this shameful act.

The heavy smoker, should learn this object lesson from the cigarette and wean himself from this terrible heaven-closing, death-hastening, shame-causing, life-shortening, disease-producing evil habit. He should develop Vairagya by looking at the ash and by reflecting thus. "This body will be reduced to ashes. It will pass away without a moment's notice. I must strive ceaselessly to attain the Imperishable wherein alone lies the supreme undying bliss. What a shameful act I am repeating again and again. I have become a slave of this terrible habit. I waste my time and energy. I waste my money uselessly. If I spend this in charitable acts, my heart will be purified and I will attain the final emancipation. Many poor persons will be benefited. I have to hide myself during smoking when I see respectable persons. My conscience pricks. My mouth stinks. People who do not smoke cannot bear this stink. I hurt their feelings even if they do not tell anything to me."

The brain of the smoker is always smoky and clouded. He meditates frequently on smoke and cigarettes. Ultimately he becomes smoke itself. His life is as substantial as smoke itself. His words, speech and actions have only the weight of smoke. His mind is saturated with smoke all throughout the day. Instead of meditating on God the poor man meditates on cigarettes and smoke every five minutes. Had he spent in contemplation of God the time he wasted in smoking, he would have become God himself. Now he remains as stinky, useless, devoid of vitality and lifeless as smoke itself. What a poor deluded soul!

There are people who spend Rs. 500 per month or more in smoking only! Yet they move about preaching economy to the masses. They stand for equal status and equal treatment, independence and freedom. They want to ameliorate the condition of the poor masses of the country. What a deplorable state! They are misusing God's trust. In the next birth they will be born as poor people and suffer from poverty. They will die of starvation.

The smoke that is sent as a puff delightfully with a twisted mouth in a fashionable manner vanishes in a moment. Where has it gone? It is not lost altogether. It has assumed a subtle form. You cannot see it by the physical eyes. But it does exists. It pervades all round you. You can behold it by some other means. This reminds you that the

Lord is all-pervading and exists in this world like the invisible subtle smoke and you can see Him through the eye of intuition in Nirvikalpa Samadhi or Super-conscious state.

A smoker cannot work vigorously in the absence of his pipe or *Hukkah* or cigarette. He gets headache and depression. He is confused and bewildered. He has become an absolute slave of tobacco. What a sad plight! That glorious Purusha who is identical with the Eternal; who is omnipotent, omniscient, who is the Lord of all senses, who is the witness of the intellect, has degenerated himself into an animal with brutal instincts and qualities and a slave of tobacco. Is this not a lamentable state?

Friends! Just imagine for a while to what all petty things you are a slave. People say that a man cannot serve two masters. But you are a slave to tobacco, tea, coffee, women, wealth, children, the employer, lust, anger, greed, petty-mindedness, jealousy and a host of other ailments. Is not freedom your birthright? Real freedom is freedom from all the above evil traits. Real freedom is attainment of Atmajnana. Why should any nation boast of independence and freedom so long as her people are subject to various defects? There is no nation in this world that can claim to be independent in the real sense of the term. Political independence is no independence at all. Butter and jam will only bind you faster to the wheel of Samsara. Try to realise God and gain the real independence.

Smoking is a mere habit. It is a vile imitation. It is not at all a necessity. It is a loose luxury. Just think of its origin. It was imported from America to England by Sir Francis Drake. He caught this queer habit from America. On his return to his native country one day he was smoking tobacco lying on the easy chair with a newspaper in his hand. His servant, astonished at the new phenomena of smoke emanating from Drake's mouth, poured a bucket of water over his head to put off the fire which he thought was devouring his master. Drake narrated the real facts to his servant. Gradually the smoke devil spread from one corner to the other of this globe. Now it has become like the

All-pervading *Atma*. There is no place, no village, no house without smoke, *beedi* or cigarette. Just imagine how habit spoils the whole world. This is new habit. Where was smoking of cigarettes a few centuries ago?

Can a slave of tobacco accomplish glorious tasks in this world, when he has not got the will-power and strength to overcome even this little habit? Maya works through habits. Habit is second nature. Conquer this evil habit and gain independence.

May Lord grant you strength to conquer this evil! May you all practise the spiritual smoking and get established in your own all-blissful Self, wherein there is neither craving nor desire!

7. STORY OF DOSAI SANGAM

United we stand; divided we fall. Union is strength. A *Sangam* or league is necessary for the building up of a nation. An association is essential for propagating religious, social, industrial, economical, political ideas and for cultural development. It must be properly organised by earnest selfless workers. Then only will the *Sangam* be stable.

"*Sangam*" means an association. *Dosai* is a kind of round cake prepared in South India for morning and evening tiffin. It is highly nutritious and very delicious too. The Bengalis, Punjabees, Hindustanees, and the European too like this. It is made up of a paste of black gram and rice. Suffcient water is added. It is poured over the frying pan and then spread with a flat spoon. The size is that of an ordinary bread that is eaten in Northern India. It is eaten with some *Chutnie*. When the paste is poured over the hot pan it produces the sound of "sayee". Hence the significant name "Dosayee".

The *Sangam* was started in 400 B.C. by a poor Brahmin named Ramakrishna Iyer in Madura. One day there was neither rice nor Dhal in his house. He had some rice flour only. He was very hungry. He made a thin paste of the flour, poured over the pan and made some cakes. But he did not relish it much as it was very hard. Necessity is the mother of invention. Man invents several things to satisfy his palate. On the second day he added some flour of black gram. Then the cake was soft and delicious. Then he opened a small hotel and sold these cakes. He made much money and became a very rich man. He opened several hotels in the neighboring districts. Thereupon several others also learnt the recipe of the famous *dosai* and started hotels throughout South India. The *Dosai Sangam* has branches all over the world now. It has penetrated even into the interior of forests. Once a European Military Officer entered a thick forest and hoisted his flag and said, "Hail, Hail, Union Jack." He thought within himself that he was the only man in the solitary place. A Malabari Nayar of South India came to him from behind and said, "Good morning, Sir, *chuda chuda* (hot) *dosai* and coffee, Sir! It is ready, Sir." The officer was quite astonished. Such is the glory of this *Dosai Sangam* founded by the late Ramakrishna Iyer of Madura.

Dosai can be made of pure green gram also *(Mung key dal)*. This is very healthy and sattvic. When a paste is made of rice, black gram, green gram and Bengal gram then you can prepare *"ADAI"* which is even more delicious than *DOSAI;* but it is a very heavy stuff. When the paste of Dosai is steamed in special vessel, it becomes, *"IDDALI"*, a small round cake. This is easily digestible. If anyone once tastes this, he will never forget it in his life. *Dosai* or *iddali* with *sambhar* is simply wonderful. With *"molagaipodi"* it is superfine. Sour *dosai* with *chundakai-mulagai* is very pleasing for some. I need not further describe the glory of *Iddali*. There can be no marriage or feast in South India without *Iddali*. *Dosai* forms *phalahara* during new moon days and other occasions. Brahmin widows take one meal in the daytime and take *Dosai* only at night.

Sangam is the place where two rivers meet. There is the *sangam* or *triveni* at Prayag (Allahabad). The Ganga and the Yamuna meet here. This is the most sacred spot. Kumbha Mela is held once in six or twelve years. There is the sangam in this body also. It is the *Sahasrara Chakra,* thousand-petalled lotus at the crown of the head. Here

Kundalini Sakti meets her consort, Lord Siva, when the Yogi is in Nirvikalpa Samadhi. The Yogi drinks the nectar of immortality and attains eternal bliss. He is freed from the round of births and deaths. This nectar of immortality is the real *dosai* of *Dosais*.

The rice paste of Prana is mixed with or united with the black gram paste of Apana and fried in the fire of Yoga during meditation. The Yogi eats this real celestial or divine *dosai* and remains ever blissful and crosses over the bridge of death. Jnana Deva ate this *DOSAI* only.

The Vedanti or Jnana Yogi mixes this rice paste of *viveka* (discrimination) with the black gram paste of *vairagya, shad smapat* (six virtues) and *mumukshutva* (strong yearing for liberation) fries it in the fire of wisdom and tastes the immortalising *dosai* of Brahma Jnana. Sankara and Dattatreya ate this *dosai* only.

The Bhakti Yogi makes a rice paste of *sravana, kirtan, smarana* etc. He adds nine things (practises Nava vidha Bhakti—nine modes of devotion) in preparing celestial *dosai*. This *dosai* is very delicious and aromatic. It is very pleasing to Lord Hari. Mira, Tuka Ram, Ram Das, Tulasi Das ate this *dosai* only. Rishi Narada keeps this *dosai* only in his pocket when he journeys through the three worlds, for his breakfast and lunch.

O Man! Enough, enough of this *dosai* of rice paste and black gram paste. You have taken this in abundance. Now taste this celestial *dosai* of *Bhava Samadhi,* the divine *dosai* of Brahma Jnana, the Yogic *Dosai* of Asamprajnata Samadhi!

8. PHILOSOPHY OF BEARD

Beard gives good personality to those who lack in personality. Some keep beard to save money. They need not pay anything to a barber. Some keep beard to command respect and get money.

Beard protects a man from danger. It protected Sri Subhash Chandra Bose when he was in difficulties by converting him into Zia-ud-Din. He must be ever thankful to this beard. Sometimes certain criminals also move about with a beard to avoid being detected.

There should be at least some grey hairs in the middle or in some corner. Only then will the beard show some signs of wisdom. Ordinary black beard in young people is showy and gay. It presents a merry making appearance. There is not much of wisdom or saintliness. A long grey beard is a veteran who has real knowledge, who is tall and stalwart, adorns him and gives him a majestic appearance. It has got its own charm and magnetic aura.

Some Sannyasins and Sadhus are very much attached to their beard. It is their be-all and end-all. One Sadhu came to me for taking Sannyasa. He said to me, "Swamiji! Initiate me into Sannyasa, but I cannot remove my beard. I have kept this for the last thirty years." Mark here! How greatly this Sadhu is attached to his beard! Maya is very powerful. It takes various forms and deludes people in diverse ways.

There is great convenience in keeping a beard. You need not be anxious to go in search of a barber. You can avoid the cuts of a blunt knife of a blunt barber. It will give you the appearance of a great saint also. But there is great inconvenience and difficulty here also. Maya never spares anybody. You will have to apply oil and soap or curd to the beard daily and comb the beard very often. You will have to keep a mirror and a comb always in your pocket. Have you not seen the ever-ready comb of a Sikh brother in the tuft of his head? Further there is great trouble and difficulty when you take your food. Great portion of the curd and Dhall stick to the moustache and beard. Time is wasted in cleaning them again and again. When you take your food, you will have to adjust the beard and moustache again and again. The bearded people know very well that their beard is a great nuisance to them and yet they cling to it and have great attachment to it. This is Maya. This is delusion. It is better not to keep a beard. You will be ever clean. You can avoid the itching and scratching in summer.

Have you not heard of the nose-cut members of the "Nose Cut Yoga School?" Similar is the case with the Beard

School of Yoga. Man is a creature of vile imitation. If one man grows beard those who surround him also gradually put on beard. Beard growing is as infectious as Typhoid.

Beard is secondary distinguishing sex mark. The harmony that is generated by the testes is the cause for this beard. If the testes is extracted, there will be no growth of beard. If the ovaries are extracted in a female and the testicular harmone is injected in her system, she will also develop a fine moustache and beard. Then you can call your aunt an uncle. Sometimes uncle also can become aunt. There had been many instance of sex-transformation. This clearly shows that everything is unreal in this world. It is all mental creation and mental jugglery. In this evanescent world there is nothing but sex and ego. Root yourself in the unchanging noumenon or the Eternal, which is bodiless, and sexless and be ever happy.

What is this beard after all? It is a little modification of Akasa Tattva. It is the seat for psoriasis, lice, ringworm and tinea. When it is shaved and thrown out, it is disgusting. No one will touch it and yet man loves it, clings to it. It pains him to part with it. His attention is there day-in and day-out. He turns it, twists, lubricates it, colours it and thinks much of it. This is his daily Pooja or worship.

May you all attain that bodiless, sexless, beardless Brahman, ever pure, ever blissful by forgetting the body and the beard, which is a great distracter!!

9. PSEUDO—VEDANTIN

Look! Mark! And Watch!
There goes the Pseudo-Vedantin!
He shaved his head,
He coloured himself the cloth.

He has no Guru,
He has no initiation,
He is a Svayamprakash Swami,
He is a self-made Guru.

He repeats Sivoham, Sivoham,
When he sees the householders,
Closes his eyes,
And sits on Padmasan.

He recites a few sentences,
From Vichar Sagar,
And Pancha Dasi too;
And calls himself a Bharati or Giri,
Puri or Saraswati.

You can see him
In all Kumba Melas
In all Bhandaras,
He knows the dates of Bhandaras
Off all Mutts and Ashrams.

This itself will help you,
To discriminate
To know the real Vedantin,
To be vigilant and careful.

This is a world of three Gunas,
There will be always pseudo-vedantins.
They exist
To glorify the real Vedantins.

10. IMPOTENT VEDANTIN

He is an impotent Vedatin,
Who always complains of Vikshep,
Who is easily upset
When he sees a big crowd;
When he lives in the bustle of a city.
When he beholds a bevy of ladies

He is an impotent Vedantin,
Who is afraid of work,

Who cannot do any work,
Who hates work.

He is an impotent Vedantin.
Who cannot concentrate
When there is noise,
Who is upset easily
When he is not respected,
When he is not given a special seat,
And special food.

He is an impotent Vedantin,
Who has no sympathy,
Who is not serving.
When one is in distress,
But simply says,
"Everything is my own self.
"Sarvam Kalvidam Brahma
This world is unreal."

He is an impotent Vedantin,
And Pseudo-Vedantin too,
Who says and smiles,
When a house is on fire,
"Everything is unreal,
The world is Lila,
This is also my Lila."
But who is not helping a bit
In the extinguishing of fire.

He is an impotent Vedantin,
Who says
'A Jnani will have no powers'.
'Sri Vasishta distinctly says,
'A Jnani will have all powers,
Through Sat-Sankalpa.'
He is an impotent Vedantin,

Who is not helpful to world,
Who has not done something grand
Which no one has done,
Like Sri Sankara, Buddha and Yajnavalkya.
But simply says,
'Who is to help whom?
Who is to serve whom?
Who is to talk to whom?
There is no world,
In the three periods of time',
But who wants all comforts.

He is an impotent Vedantin,
Who simply gossips on Vedanta,
Who vomits something he crammed,
But who cannot talk a few sentences,
And who cannot write something beautiful.

11. LIP—VEDANTIN

He talks much on Vedanta,
He is fond of tall talk,
He gossips and poses,
He is fond of pedantry.

There are some flowers,
With beautiful colours,
But they have no scent.
He is like these flowers.

He talks and talks,
But does not act accordingly,
Oneness is unknown to him.
He discusses and fights.

He condemns and criticises,
He quotes scriptures,
You can see him on every platform,

He will vomit some nonsense,
He will condemn Bhakti
He will belittle Karma.

He will talk of Samadhi,
But ethics is unknown to him
He is full of lies,
He backbites and vilifies.

He will catch fish,
In the Ganga,
To satisfy his palate,
And say 'Nainam Chindanti Sastrani'
'Swords would not pierce the soul.'
Now you can clearly diagnose,
Who is an Impotent Vedantin,
A pseudo-Vedantin,
And lip Vedantin,
I leave it for you to judge now.

12. REAL VEDANTIN

He is a real sage,
He is full of wisdom,
He is silent and peaceful,
He is radiant and joyful.

He never asks anything,
He gives and gives,
He transforms others
He elevates and inspires.

He is a veritable God on the earth,
He is humble and simple.
In his mere presence
All doubts are cleared.

He is free from anger and egoism,

He teaches through silence,
He is one with all,
He beholds the Self everywhere.

He is full of mercy,
He bears insult and injury,
He is truthful and cordial,
He is above body-consciousness.

13. DIVINE INJECTION S.B. 40.

This is also known as "Anti-Asuric Injection—S.B. 40" The unregenerate man is an essence of hundred black cobras and hundred black scorpions. A cobra has venom in its fangs or teeth. A scorpion has venom in its tail. But man has venom all over his body. His essential nature is to hurt others some way or other all the twentyfour hours of the day.

Rude behaviour, harsh speech, unkind acts entirely eclipse one's good qualities.

You do wrong actions and then say, "I apologise ," "Please excuse me". You have done like this thousand and one times and yet your unregenerate nature remains the same. You repeat it again and again.

Live under a Guru. Obey him. Serve him. Rectify your defects. Pray and do Japa. Then only will your old Asuric nature change.

Have rigorous self-punishment. Fast entirely for a day or two. Do plenty of Japa. Pray fervently. Then only will your old unregenerate demoniacal nature change. Or, stand in the market-place. Admit your faults openly, and allow a scavenger to shoe you with his old shoes 40 times. This is the best method to correct and improve yourself. This is most potent injection to cure this disease instantaneously.

Injection S.B. 40 means *Shoe-beating 40 times.*

14. SPIRITUAL LUMBAGO

Spiritual Lumbago is a more formidable disease than ordinary lumbago. Lumbago is rheumatism of the muscles of the hips or loins. There is severe pain in the lumbar region. The patient finds it difficult to walk freely and bend down his body. Sometimes the pain becomes very severe. He will have to remain in bed. He cannot turn on the sides. The pain is like electric shock.

Lumbago is due to pride of learning yoga practices, wearing orange-coloured robe, Mahantship, lecturing capacity on Yoga, Vedanta etc., acquisition of some Yoga powers etc. Minute particles of pride are deposited in the lumbar region. He who suffers from spiritual limbago cannot bend his body and do full prostration to elderly Sannyasins, elderly people, and to the deities in a temple. He cannot bend his neck also. Just as in rheumatism, the pain shifts from one joint to another joint, the pride particles move from the hips to the neck also.

This sort of lumbago is found in dry Pundits, dry intellectual people, rich people and big officers too. They also cannot bend their necks and body. They cannot do full prostrations to anybody, and to the Lord in the temples also. They think that they are the Lord themselves.

The best injections to cure this spiritual lumbago are B.F. (Bank Failure) and I.D. (Incurable Disease). There two injections will open their eyes and soften their stiff muscles of their hips and necks, and force them to run to the Swamis for any Himalayan herb or Booty or any Lakshmi Mantra to remove their poverty. Divine Injection S.B. 40 is more powerful than B.F. and I.D. Please try this once. It will effect instantaneous cure. It is a specific indeed!

Prostration with Bhava, faith and devotion will bestow on you fame, long life, joy and spiritual strength. It is an *anga* or limb of Nava Vidha Bhakti. When Uddhava was not able to comprehend the deep truths of Yoga and Vedanta, Lord Krishna said, "O Uddhava, I shall give you a very easy method for attaining Me. See Me in all beings. Prostrate before all. Prostrate before an ass, and an outcaste even. See Me in them. You will soon attain Me. There is no doubt of this."

O ignorant man! What will you gain puffed up with pride? Pride will bring your downfall and destruction. Be humble. What you have learnt is handful only. What you have not learnt is oceanful.

May you all be free from pride! May your hearts be filled with humility! Glory to B.F. and I.D. and S.B. 40 Injections!!

15. THE KNOWLEDGE OF THE LAD

One moonlit night, after supper, young Soni pressed his mother Kamalji to tell him a very interesting story. Kamala caressed young Soni with motherly affection and began to narrate the following story:—

Once upon a time, in the city of Kalinga, there was a famous and renowned printing press called Noman's Press. Mr. Noman was its sole proprietor. The capital invested for the starting of the press was zero crores of rupees.

The press was equipped with types of different fonts and had very beautiful faces which were all made of superior molten clay. Thus the type-foundry section of the press stood unrivalled for its production. The ink used for printing was pure acqua mixed with lime. There were a number of machines well fitted with up-to-date mechanism. They were all manufactured out of strong cast bamboo sticks well burnt to ashes. The compositors, proof-readers and the other staff of the press were, without exception, all blind.

Equipped with such an up-to-date and well-organised machinery and staff, the press earned goodwill and fame which reached the three worlds—earth, heaven and the nether world. The proprietor, Mr. Noman, became even wealthier than Kubera, the Lord of wealth. Even the Gods envied his wealth and prosperity. Lacs and crores of books with 000, 000, 000 pages were printed in the press daily. Every sheet of paper of the book had only one side. The press flourished for crores of centuries of a moment's duration of Noman's mental world, serving the humanity with its valuable publications.

Your Soni was very happy to hear the captivating story and believed every word of his mother as truth.

Such is the reality of the world of sensual happiness and the fate of Mr. Noman will be shared by those who expect happiness from sensual objects of the world.

16. BEST CEMENT

Dalmia's cement is good.
But three "B.B.E." is more famous.
Yet "R.P.M." cement is the best.
For it is the Divine brand.
Harder than cement is ego.
Break this through Atma Vichar.
Love is indeed the best cement.
To cement broken hearts.
Purchase this though it is dear,
Because it is the best.
It is largely manufactured,
In the heart-mills of India's Rishis.
The ingredients of this rare cement
Are Rati, Prem and Mahabhav.

17. FOUNTAIN PEN

They say, Waterman's pen is ideal,
But Waterbird is liked by many.
Some prefer Parker.
Parker is very costly.
A fountain pen is very convenient.
It adorns your pocket.
You can write speedily.
But all these are worthless.
Some times they become constipated.
You cannot write.
At other times they get diarrhoea,
And spoil your papers,
Your fingers too.
They cause great nuisance.
Throw these showy pens.
Use ordinary pens.
You can save money.
You can be at ease.

What does the fountain pen teach?
It teaches,
This world is as hollow,
As its barrel.

18. KNOWLEDGE OF A CHILD

Once a mother narrated
A story to her child.
He heard it as if quite true,
Just as ignorant men take this world as real.

There was a rich king in Sourashtra.
He had neither dominion nor wealth,
Neither attendant nor palace.
He held the scepter of a blade of grass.

He married the handsome daughter
Of the Maharani Zero
And begot five sons,
Four not born, one not conceived.
He once moved in the air for shooting,
With the help of an iron girder.
He shot a big elephant and a tiger.
And brought them to his city of Void.
He built a wonderful palace,
Of carbon dioxide and sulphurated hydrogen,
For four lacs of rupees minus six lacs,
And lived there when he died.

He took a medicine.
Made of buffalo's egg,
Mosquito's milk and the juice of rock.
He was cured of the terrible disease-Lingual diarrhoea.

He was once indeed very thirsty,
And drank the fresh water,

Of the desert of Sahara,
From a bottomless bucket.

He went to take bath in a river,
Which had no water.
He took there ten dips,
And got quite refreshed.

He was a very great devotee,
But had no faith in God,
In God's Name and His mercy,
And he wanted everything but God.

This world is as true as this story.
Beware of Maya's charms and deception.
Brahman alone is real.
Know Him and be free.

19. BOY BECOMES A GIRL

Boy becomes a girl.
He develops new things.
Old things withers;
He feels shy.

The girl also becomes a boy.
She develops moustache.
The voice breaks.
Her qualities change.

But they cannot develop
The real inner sex-mechanism.
The boy cannot develop ovaries.
The girl cannot get testes.

Real sex organ is ovary
And the testes,

But not the external things.
This is a freak of nature.
This teaches,
That the world is illusory,
Sex is a mental creation.

There is something beyond sex.
It is sexless pure Brahman.
It is bodiless transcendental Atman,
Full of Bliss and Knowledge.
Realise this Atman,
And be ever free.

20. MOUSTACHE LADY

He who is timid,
He who is afraid of a cat
When he sees it at night,
Is a moustache Lady.

He who is afraid of Nivritti,
Renunciation or Tyaga,
Is indeed a lady,
Though he has moustache.

The world abounds with
Moustache ladies and weaklings.
This Atma cannot be attained
By weak and timid men.

Even ladies like Sulabha,
Madalasa and Maitreyi
Have attained Self-realisation.
O! moustache ladies!

Give up timidity.
Draw inspiration from them,
And become absolutely fearless.

21. TEST-TUBE BABY

This is a new thing indeed.
Scientists are ever busy,
In inventing new things,
And astounding the world.

Healthy and intelligent,
Men and women,
Are selected by the medical board.
The seed is carried
In an aeroplane.

The seed is injected.
It is reported,
The children are,
Very healthy and intelligent,

It is a laudable scheme
For bringing a new race.
But the half-brother will marry,
The half-sister

Who is the father
For the new born babe?
The world will mock at him
And call him a test-tube "Tom".

This is against nature.
He may not possess
Brilliant spiritual traits,
As he is a laboratory production only
Like H-Two, S.O. Four..

22. SPIRITUAL SHAVING

There was an innocent fawn,
Standing on a pleasant lawn.

The lawn was ever green,
With grass tenderest ever seen.
Sweet aroma pervaded
The lawn and its surroundings.

Dew drops dripped from the sky;
Like honey from the bee-hive.

The moon was shining all along,
Shedding its sylvan rays of charm.

Everywhere was calmness and quietude,
Undisturbed stillness and serenity.

The fawn was lost for a while,
In the Natural Beauty.

It stood motionless for a while
Free from fear and anxiety.

Suddenly it was disturbed
By the flash of folly.
It sped from the spot
With lightning speed.
It was really enchanted
By the picturesque scenery.

This too lasted for a while
And the deer became perturbed.

A thundering roar from the distance,
Agitated the mild deer.

The deer fled from the spot too,
Fell in the bush gasping.

There are fawns and deers
Among people, young and old.

They have no settled programme of life.
They have no strong will-power too.

They desert their family and home,
And run away pell-mell.

Still they possess Vairagya
And coolly slip in an Ashram.

This Vairagya helps them to realise,
The benefits of an Ahsram-life.

But Poorva Samskaras goad them
To their good old attachments.
Pride, prejudice and jealousy,
Possess them virulently.

They pick petty quarrels,
And lastly lead themselves out.

Yet this Vairagya is not vanquished,
Still it spurs them indeed.

They enter many Ashrams and peep through
Again and again fights and quarrels.

Meanwhile there goes on fierce fight,
Inside their mind and heart.

Powerless and spiritless fails Vairagya.
Most of them become worldly again.

This is all due to folly.
Aspirants! Don't be silly.

Years and years may roll on.
Yet you will be in the same position.

Devolop real Vairagya.
Be unshaken by circumstances.

Develop mental poise.
Never give vent to anger.

Curbing evil qualities,
Is not an easy joke.

You have to try, and try again,
Until at last you succeed.

The hairs that you grow on your cheek,
Do not stop with a single shave.

They grow, grow, and grow again,
You have to shave, shave and shave again.

The hairs of the vices are deep-rooted.
They can't be removed by Panama or Gillette.

Sharpen your razor of real Vairagya.
Commence shaving at Brahmamuhurta.

The hairs on the chin,
Can be removed in a minute.

But it will consume your whole life
To annihilate the evil qualities.

Do not be deluded.
Do not be puffed up.

May you have true enlightenment!
May you have realisation in this birth!

28. CHANDRABHAGA AND MONKEY

Chandrabhaga is a very sacred river in Maharashtra. The famous Pandarpur, sweet abode of Lord Vithala, is situated on the bank of this holy river. There is also another turbulent river named Chandrabhaga in Rishikesh. I will speak a few words about the mischievous nature of this boisterous Chandrabhaga. There is a *raison deter* (cause for existence) for all the objects of the world created by the Lord. Tree exists to give shade to the travellers and yield fruits to the people. Cow exists to give milk to the people. But there appears to be no *raison deter* cause for the existence of Chandrabhaga and monkey.

Does the monkey do any good to the people. It does always harm. It bites people, takes away things from the house and does all sorts of mischief which can hardly be imagined. It takes away the shoes, tears the clothes, etc. it snatches away your edible stuffs from your hands even you are in the train in Ayodhya, when you take your food in the dining hall of Ananda Kutir, even if people stand with raised sticks. No part of it is useful after its death.

The course of this mischievous and boisterous river has been turned for the last four years. It runs more towards the Muni-ki-reti side. This is a very broad river. It is like an ocean. It causes a terrible roar after a heavy rain. Like the monkey it does no good to people. It is absolutely dry during summer and winter, but appears in a very virulent and formidable form like the foaming Kaali of the Himalayas which you will see during your trip to Kailas.

This year (1946) some have died while crossing it. It is not very deep but the current is very forcible. There are big stones. It makes you roll and do somersault and takes you to Ganga Sagar and gives you Jala Samadhi instantaneously.

It has swept away this year some big buildings and many thatched Kutir of Sadhus. It may join after some years with its old parent current and may devastate the whole Jadi and a portion of Rishikesh. There is such impending danger.

Sometimes pilgrims and inhabitants of Muni-ki-reti cross it on the elephant's back. But sometimes the elephant also slips its footsteps and there is still more danger.

Postal communication is stopped. Ananda Kutir people cannot get the bundles of the DIVINE LIFE magazine. They are now lying in the Viswanath Bhag. There is Postal strike also. Without realising the difficulties, the subscribers are sending daily complaints. There was difficulty in getting paper. June and July issues are ready for dispatch. Please wait patiently. Please develop an understanding heart. If there is some delay in the dispatch of the magazine, know that there is some reason and cause for the unusual delay. Do not agitate yourself and the office by posting frequent complaints. Let the Postal strike be over. You will get both the issues in one dispatch.

There is the *raison deter* for the existence of the monkey. It keeps you alert and vigilant. It helps you to develop these virtuous qualities. It reminds you of the noble and exalted personage Lord Hanuman. It reminds you of the great works done by the band of monkeys in constructing the bridge of Rameshwar. It puts you in mind of the army of monkeys who served Lord Rama and the Ramayana in which their works are glorified. Devotees of Lord Hanuman should feed them with gram, etc., at least on Saturdays, the day set apart for the worship of Lord Hanuman. Many devotees are already doing this without any break. This is done regularly in Anandakutir. Pilgrims also distribute gram for the monkeys. Lord Hanuman is pleased if you feed them. The monkey reminds you that behind the name and form, there is the Sat-chit-ananda essence and that you should realise this essence by giving up the names and forms.

There is a *raison deter* for the existence of this boisterous Chandrabhaga also. It bespeaks of the glory and omnipotence of the Lord, its Creator. Many coolies get some money by helping the pilgrims to cross the river. They are supported during the rainy season. Some Sadhus who are shut out from getting their alms from the Kalikambli-wala kshettar come for Bhiksha to Anandakutir and thus purify the Ananda Kshettra and the abode of the Ashram.

O gracious Maharaja of Tehri! Be kind to construct a bridge immediately. The sufferings of the pilgrims and the inhabitants of Muni-ki-reti are very great, indeed. It is beyond description.

This is a world of difficulties, contradictions catastrophes and calamities. You are surrounded by all sorts of perils, diseases and dangers. If the flood disaster ends, cholera epidemic will start. The first great war ended and the second great war started. The second has ended and still there is no peace. Famine is raging everywhere. The number of atomic bombs is increasing on silently. Scientists are sleepless. Uranium atoms are ceaselessly bombarded. Each party whishes to possess more atomic bombs. Atomic bombs is their goal, ideal, centre and God. There is no end for human troubles on this earth-plane.

O man! Try to get rid of this body and birth. Strive ceaselessly to attain this end. Become bodiless and birthless. Attain this through Yoga, enquiry, meditation, devotion and selfless service and enjoy immortality and eternal bliss for ever. Cross this boisterous Chandrabagha, formidable river of Samsara (worldly existence) by controlling this monkey mind and become absolutely fearless, happy, free, perfect and independent.

He who dwells in this Chandrabhaga and monkey, who

is within this Chandrabhaga and monkey, whose body is this Chandrabhaga and monkey, whom this Chandrabhaga and monkey do not know, who rules this Chandrabhaga and monkey from within, is Thy Self, Inner Ruler, Immortal. Glory to this Inner Ruler!

Know Him, realise Him and be free.

24. A COMPLAINT TO BRAHMA

O Omniscient Lord!
O Omnipotent Isvar!
Salutations unto Thee.
I have a small complaint
Against Thee.
Hear me, patiently, my Lord.
You already know
About the work at Ananda Kutir.
Young aspirants full of vigour
Work very hard indeed.
There are still arrears of work.
I will have night shifts also.
But yet the hours in a day
Are not sufficient.
"24"—This is too little.
Make it "48" now.
Why have you not done this
In the beginning
When Nada-bindu vibrated?
This is my strong and just complaint.

25. THE STORY OF A LADDU

I am a laddu. I am very sweet and delicious. All love me very much. I am liked very much by children. Their mouth waters when they see me and hear my name. There is no big feast on a grand scale without me. All devour me voraciously.

I make a crying child laugh and dance in joy. I give life to a weak man. I become fat and flesh and shine in the cheeks and skin. People take great care of me. They keep me in a good boxes and almirahs and big costly vessels. I increase the value of sugar, ghee and flour of gram.

The Indweller in me is Atman or God. I cannot live without Him. If people love Him in the same way, as they love me, they would have attained eternal bliss long, long ago.

26. THE SECRET OF "BADA"

"Bada" is an eatable. It is prepared out of Bengal-gram, "Bada" means also big or great in Hindi Language. One day "Bada" said, "You know how I became Bada? It was like this", and narrated its story.

"I was fat and plumpy gram in the beginning. I was in the fields free and independent. I was proud of my fat body. I thought there was none equal to me in all the worlds. One day the farmer came and cut me down with a sharp sickle. I fell down and was then severely beaten by the coolies of the farmer. My outer skin was removed. Then I was thrashed in the thrashing pan. I was then sealed in the grocers shop within the dark godown inside a gunny bag for six months. One fine Sunday morning I was taken out and brought in Lalaji's house. There the Lalaji asked his cook to soak me in the water for 24 hours. I was then taken out from water and crushed well with salt, chillies and ginger between two big stones till such time my shape and name totally vanished. I was then fried in the boiling ghee. Now I have become 'Bada'. My very name makes your mouth water. I am indispensable in all big feasts and parties. Such is my glory. All this is on account of my ungrudging sacrifice that I underwent for such a long time. I completely effaced myself." So saying Bada concluded his autobiography. This story of Bada should put you in the right path and you also should become really a "Bada Admi" (great man).

27. THIS IS MAYA

A Man is very, very lean
But he always thinks "When can I become fat".
He tries all sorts of methods

He drinks plenty of ghee
He swallows tons of butter
He gulps maunds of Cod-liver oil.

He rubs all sorts of oil on his cheek and body
He shampoos and massages
He approaches many Sadhus
And takes all sorts of Bhuti and herbs
But he still remains in the same condition.
This is Maya.

A man is very, very fat
But he always thinks "When can I become lean"
He also tries all sorts of medicines
But he remains in the same state
He cannot give up his ghee.
This is Maya.

A doctor thinks "A Judge is more happy"
A Judge thinks "A Professor is more happy",
A professor thinks "A Business man is more happy"
A business man thinks, "A Raja is more happy",
No one is really happy in this world.
This is Maya.
A knower of Brahman alone is really happy.

A man has really nothing,
But he thinks he is a rich man.
A man is really a fool,
But he thinks he is a wise man.
A woman is really ugly,
But she thinks she is a great devotee,
Maya is an illusory power of the Lord.
Obtain the grace of the Lord,

Through self-surrender and devotion,
You can easily conquer Maya.

Maya intoxicates, veils,
And clouds the understanding,
She hides the real,
And makes the unreal
Appears as real.
She is cunning woman,
She is very crafty and diplomatic.

28. PHILOSOPHY OF SHIRT AND HAT

Nambiar presented a Military Shirt to Swamiji. Swamiji put on and gave a military salute to the inmates. Swamiji is always humorous. He radiates joy and strength through educative humour. He said, "Military shirt makes a man military minded. It induces him to fight. Every object has its own association. A rosary makes you remember God. It instills Sattvic divine ideas in your mind. If you hold Gita or Bible in your hand, it will generate divine ideas in your mind. Select Sattvic objects for elevating your mind."

Some visitor forgot to take his hat. He left it in the dining hall. Swamiji put it on his head and saluted the inmates by raising the hat. He then put the hat on the table and said, "O Hat? Maker of Babus and gentlemen! Instiller of pride and vanity in the hearts of people; Salutations unto Thee. Thou art Maya's child that deludes the poor, ignorant Jiva. Thou art nothing. Thou art a piece of card-board after all, with a piece of cloth over it and yet Thou maketh even a beggar a gentleman, for the time being, for five minutes. He walks with high steps and grand lordly gait and thinks that he is the Lord or Baron even though he has nothing to eat. What charm and power are there in thee! You stiffen the egoism and make him say when he is angry, "Do you know who I am? His gait changes when he puts on the hat. You strengthen the Deha-adhyasa, identification with the body. Thank you very much. You saved me. You did not dare to approach me. You had no attraction for me. O Hat! Continue thy work vigorously, and delude the pitiable Jivas. You cannot do much in India now. The Interim Government has come. Now all go with ordinary clothes to the Secretariate. Goodbye, Hat. Again salutations, as you are the child of my Mother, MAYA!

29. EQUAL VISION

The state of equal vision is much misunderstood. Equal vision is with reference to the one common consciousness or Atman or the immortal soul in all beings. Giving apples or grapes to the pigs is not equal vision. They will not like them. They will like only their own delicious food. A Jivanmukta who has equal vision will not embrace all women who pass on the road saying "I have equal vision in man and woman. "He will not walk on his head saying, "I have equal vision in legs and head." He will not eat faecal matter saying, "I have equal vision in rice and faecal matter." He will not eat through the anus saying, I have equal vision in anus and the mouth."

Body is mistaken for Atman; licentiousness is practised in the name of Vedantic equal vision by people of small understanding.

The Sruti declares, "He who sees all beings in the Self (Atman) and the Self in all beings, shrinks not from anything thereafter. He who sees the One Atman or the Supreme Self in all beings, how can there be delusion or grief for him, how can he be afraid of anything?" (Isavasya Upanishad: 6,7). "The Self harmonised by Yoga sees the Atman in all beings, and all beings in the Self; everywhere he sees the same." (Gita: VI.29). "Sages behold the one humility, a cow, an elephant and even a dog and an outcaste and thus have equal vision." (Gita: V.18).

Behold the one Atman in all beings. This is equal vision.

You can have Bhavana-Advaitam. You cannot have Kriya-Advaitam. If there are three seers of milk and if there are twenty inmates in an Ashram, the three seers should be given to the six sick persons only.

30. GADAPPARAI OR DURMAT NYAYA

Sri Gouri Prasad, M.A.,L.L.B., Deputy Collector asked "Swamiji! I find sometimes repetitions in some of your books."

Swamiji replied: It is Gadapparai or Durmat Nyaya. Nyaya means analogy. Gadapparai in Tamil is the big iron rod used by the labourers in digging the earth. By frequent hitting by Gadapparai big stones are broken into pieces. By continual use of Durmat the foundation is rendered stronger. 'Durmat' is a Hindi term. Similarly repetition gives strength. The ideas are firmly grounded in the mind. It is beneficial for the intelligent and dull-witted person also. The Rishis of yore who brought forth the Upanishads have also repeated the same sentences many a time. They took recourse to the Gadapparai Durmat Nyaya. The following are some such instances:

1. "Andham Tamah Pravishanti"etc. (Isa. Up. 9) also occurs in Brih. Up. 4.4.10.

2. "Na Tatra Suryo Bhati" etc. (Katha Up. 5,15) occurs in Mund. Up. 2.2.10.

3. "Yada Sarve Pramuchyante" etc., (Katha Up. 6.14) occurs in Brith. 4.4.7.

Uddalaka repeated "Tat Twam Asi" nine times in order to drive into Swetaketu the Highest Truth. Thus there are countless instances.

Gouri Prasad, "Thank you Swamiji. I now realise and understand the importance of repetitions."

31. BRAHMA-JNANA RESEARCH PHARMACY

Ananda Kutir

(RISHIKESH, Himalayas.)

Telegrams:	Para Brahman.	*Consulting hours:*
Telephone:	I	AT ALL TIMES.

OM

32. Tat Twam asi.

Consulting Doctor: Dr. BRAHMAN

Codes	J.M. (Niralambapuri).
Prasthana Traya	(Jivanmukta).
Brahma Sutras	P.N. (Brahmapuri).
Ten Upanishads	(Brahmanishta).
Gita	B.L. (Mt. Kailas).
	Brahmaleen
	(Specialist in Brahma Vidya).
BRAHMAN'S PATENT	Brahma Rasayana
	(Extra Strong).
Prescription	000000000
Name	Brahman Om.
Sex	Sexless Atman.
Disease	Birth and death.
X-'Ray findings	Moola Ajnana
	(ignorance) in Karana
	Sarira (causal body)
	and Vasanas (desires)
	in the mind.
Diet	Sattvic food (pure diet)
Caste	Self.
Age	Eternity.

33. RECIPE (TAKE THOU).

Commonsense	Gr. 1.
Prudence	Gr. ½.
Self-reliance	Gr. ½.
Faith	drachm. 1.
Understanding	drachm. 1.
Patience	oz. 1.
Perseverance	oz. 6.
Resolution	lb. 1.

Vairagya (dispassion)	Q.S. (Quantity sufficient).
Iron will	oz. 8.
Tranquillity	dr. 1.
Abstraction	dr. 1.
Endurance	dr. 2.
Equanimity	dr. 4.
Syrup Mumukshutva	oz. 8.
Elixir Meditation	oz. 8.

(Fiat mixture: Moksha Rasayana)

Sig:—One tea-spoonful every two hours.
Price; INLAND; Suddha Prem and faith.
　　　FOREIGN: Simple living and high thinking.

　　　　　　　　　　　　Sd./- Dr. BRAHMAN.

34. PHILOSOPHY OF PROVERBS

Very often we run after the shadow, discarding the substance in the background. In the spiritual sense, this theory is the very root of bondage. Instead of seeking God and realising his oneness with Him, man runs after His shadow, the world. This is the cause of all misery on earth.

Even in the case of the meaning of the word "God" itself, we more often than not understanding the "Shadow" rather than the real "Substance" that is God. We concentrate so much on this unreal things that in course of time we lose consciousness of the tree, we miss the grand spectacles of the wood!

This is true of our understanding of the Scriptures, too. How often have not reformers had to thunder forth to antagonistic millions the true significance of the teaching of the prophets and saints and dispel the darkness of wrong notions that had covered up the essence! The origin of most of the religions of the world could be traced out to this sort of renaissance. The source was only one religion. In course of time, people of deluded understanding began to interpret its tenets variously and started forming parties. They split themselves into opposing camps, each owning to be the sole votaries of the real purport of the ancients' utterances. Then will arise a star who will dive deeper into the ocean of Wisdom and bring out the pearl of Truth. Some will follow him; others will still strike the discordant note. The new Seer will get together a band of followers to propagate his teachings; and these will establish a new religion. And, so the game has gone on for ages!

Besides the scriptural teachings, all religions have had the "sayings" of their prophets. These are also classed under proverbs, though these include other ideas. Those of the proverbs which have such a spiritual background have as much of deep, secret and mystical meaning as the scriptural utterances themselves. This makes the real idea which they wish to convey to be misconstrued by posterity; and often some nonsensical notes are sounded in a futile attempt to give a true rendering of this sublime music!

Let us take a few examples from the Tamil literature. There is a beautiful (and amusing as it has become nowadays) proverb which means: "When you see (the) dog, there is no stone; when you see (the) stone, there is no dog". This has come to be regarded as a remark made by some one in a light vein, or at least not in a very serious mood. The proverb is taken to convey what it literally does. A man is passing along the road in a village. Several dogs stroll about him "What a pity!" he is made to think, "There are so many dogs all about me. How I wish there was a stone near at hand, so that I could enjoy a throw at them!" During a pilgrimage the same man looks at beautiful, well-polished stones lining the banks of the Ganga; then he thinks: "What a pity, again! Here there are any number of the most lovely stones. But, not a dog to hit them with!" This is the interpretation of the vulgar. Even the serious amongst humanity nowadays will at best interpret it to mean that this proverb merely restates an old idea regarding earthly fortunes. Where money is most needed, it is usually absent; where it is already superfluous, it is found in more and more abundance. Few care to stop to think what the proverb really has to convey.

Before we proceed to examine the underlying sense of this proverb let us divert our attention to "God" visa a-vis the world. What is this world and what is God? "Brahma Satyam Jagan Mithya Jeevo Brahmaiva Na-aparah", roared the ancient seers. God alone is Truth; the world does not exist at all, they said. But, we see it!—posed the uninitiated. Yes, we see it as we see a snake in the rope; as we see water in the mirage; as we see silver in the mother-of-pearl. A man comes home from his office, tired and exhausted and as he steps into his house, he feels that he has trodden over a snake. He is not able to examine the thing in the darkness. In that weakened state, his reasoning fails him. His head reels, he is in the grip of fear. He imagines that he has been badly bitten by this snake. He staggers into the house and collapses into the nearest bed. At once a hue and cry! The man has been bitten by the snake. He almost loses consciousness. Crowds of people surround his cot. Weeping and wailing; praying and prattling; pandemonium prevails in the house. A seasoned man with flowing grey hairs of wisdom enters and shouts: "leave the way, let me examine the patient." He gets nearer the bed, and calmly examines the man. Unable to detect any signs of snake-bite, he thinks, his hands combing the long beard. "No, this can't be." He is determined! "Let me see," he says: Where did the snake bite you?" The dying man feebly answers; "Four yards away from the entrance." With a lantern in hand, the old man sets out on his errand. Of course, the snake if it had bitten him would not be stationary, still. Exactly, on the spot mentioned by the patient, there was "the snake". But the flash of lights has turned it into an old garland of flowers! Triumphantly, with that garland-snake in hand the old man returns to the death-bed and with a sagacious twitch playing on his lips, he exhibits the snake to the astounded audience. "This is, my dear man, the snake that bit you. It has no poison-fangs. So, wake up. Change your shirt which is wet with perspiration." The dying man is at once electrified and the pain and fear leave him. Brightly he gets up, embraces his saviour, and bids goodbye to the crowd!

That is what the world is. It is a superimposition on Brahman. In essence, it is not there; at least, as what it seems to be. So long as you see it in darkness, it appears as the snake. Light the lamp of wisdom and in its effulgence, the world, as such, will disappear, and you will perceive the Essence (Brahman) in all Its grandeur. Several Tamil saints have conveyed this idea in very beautiful, and sublime, verses. He who sees God, does not perceive the world made up of the five elements; and he who is engrossed in the play of this elements, is blinded to the vision of God.

To arrive at the real purport of the proverbs, we should know the context in which that proverb took its birth. Only then can we understand the sense which the letters wish to convey.

A sculptor moves around an old temple, with every one of his senses and the mind absorbed in the beautiful of the carvings on the walls of the temple. He feels the tail of a cat; ah, how beautiful it is! There, the mouth of the lion with that stone-ball inside! So, he moves from one carving to another. He takes a turn. "Lo! This huge dog! If only it jumps on me! Look at its sharp teeth; and its blood-thirsty tongue flowing out of its mouth! It is looking directly at me. Oh, my God, what am I to do now?" Perplexed, he closes his eyes. One minute passes, two, three, four. Still the dog is hesitant. "Why, probably it is chained." He throws a small stone at it. It does not move. He goes nearer. Still it stands where it was, staring at him all the time. "Why, it does not even wag its tail? Peculiar dog it must be." He goes yet nearer, and touches its tail. His whole body rocks with laughter at his own idiotic behaviour. It is made of stone! Yet, such was the workmanship, the colouring and the art that it actually looks like a live dog. This is what was meant by the poet who said: "When there is the dog, there is no stone; when there is the stone, there is no dog." When you see the dog, there was no idea that it was of stone. When you realise it is made of stone, the idea of dog vanishes! What a travesty of truth it is to superimpose all sorts of ludicrous ideas on this proverb which conveys the highest truth! When you see the diversity,

Unity disappears; and vice versa. When you realise God, world disappears; when you lose yourself in the world, you cannot realise God!

This idea is beautifully expressed in many a couplet in Tamil literature. One says; "The elephant screened the wood; and in the wood disappeared the elephant." It sounds mystic! Take an instance. A young child has an elephant made of mango-wood which he got as a present from his fond parent. A carpenter is working on the verandah. It runs to him and shows the elephant to him. "See, how big are his legs. Look at his window-like ears. Pooh! The tusks will pierce your chest." It plays with it as if it were an elephant in reality. The carpenter takes the doll in his hand and examines it. "Why, child, it is not a good one." "What, my elephant?" "Yes. It is made of mango-wood. It will get spoiled-soon." To the carpenter, it is not an elephant; but a piece of wood! Such is the difference in the attitude towards the world between the worldly man and a saint. The worldly man sees the world as a diversity, as a mixture of pleasure and pain, as a conglomeration of objects; the saint perceives the one Hidden Essence which pervades the whole universe, to him it is an "abhasa" of That Existence-Knowledge-Bliss Absolute, Brahman.

II

Now, take another proverb. Translated into English, is means. "When the 'ooru', is split, things were easy for the dancer." This word "ooru: is taken to mean "village". There once lived in a village a big zamindar who owned the entire village itself. A street-dancer used to visit the place once in a way and get rich presents from the zamindar after a performance of his art. The zamindar died, and his two sons inherited their father's property. Naturally, it was divided between the two. As happens with most of the South Indian families, they both established their own houses. Now, the street-dancer again visited the village and found the zamindar's household divided between the two brothers. He went to one of the brothers and exhibited his feats. He received rich presents from him. He then visited the other brother and gave a performance there also. This brother also gave him rich presents; but found out by and by the value of those given by his brother. Out of sheer vanity, he gave more than his brother did! Thus, whereas the dancer would have got presents only from one zamindar, he was now able to get a lion's share in view of the fact that the family was split into two. This is taken to be the real meaning of the proverb.

A moral is usually drawn from the story that families should ever try to remain united; or else some "Third party" would plunder both parties to his own advantage at the expense of both of them! When we understand the real meaning, however, we would merely laugh at such perverted explanations.

An important word in the proverb "ooru" is misunderstood to mean "a village" and a whole parable is woven round it! If we think for a while, we are sure to arrive at the correct meaning of the whole proverb. The word "ooru" has been borrowed from Sanskrit where it means "thigh".

You are probably aware of the story of Oorvasi's birth. Sage Narayana was performing severe penance in the Himalayas for innumerable years. Indra, who usually gets upset whenever a saint performs penance, wanted to foil Narayan's attempts. He sent many celestial damsels to tempt Sage Narayana. They approached him with this end in view. They danced, sang, and spread their tempting net over the saint absorbed in his Self. He sensed the mischief; opened his eyes and saw the damasels straining every one of their nerves to disturb him. He smiled at their folly! And as they were looking on, struck his right thigh with his palm. To the bewilderment of the celestials, there arose from that thigh a veritable army of the most bewitching female forms. These latter charmed Indra's messengers who fell their victims instantly. They soon forgot all about their mission and remained there itself. Indra waited, and waited. At last, despaired of the return of his missionaries, he sent some of his deputies to find out the cause of their delay. Those Devas, in their turn, were themselves the victims of Sage Narayana's creations. Indra himself came later, found out the facts. But for the Sage's grace upon him, Indra would himself have fallen a victim to the lustful looks of these women. Realising his incapacity, Indra at once fell prostrate at Narayana's feet and begged his pardon. Afraid that his own celestials would fade into insignificance if the Sage's creation were allowed to compete with them, he requested Narayana to withdraw the women that he created. The sage at once recalled all the damsels except one to enter his thigh. This one he sent with Indra. She was Urvasi—one who lived in the thigh of Narayana.

That is what "ooru" means. Now, taking this meaning of the word, let us analyse the proverb again. "Because of the separation of the thigh, it was easy for the dancer." The famous story of the Dance of Siva comes before our mind's eye. Parvathi, Lord Siva's consort, challenged her husband to a dance-competition. To establish His supremacy over her, the Lord danced for a long time. Parvathi was equally adept. She proved His equal in every respect. At last a queer idea struck Him. He raised one of His legs up and danced. No decent woman could do that without losing her chastity and proper demeanour! Parvathi reflected for a moment, and submitted. She acknowledge defeat. The proverb reminds us of this Divine Event; "Was it not because the thighs were separated, that victory was easy for the Dancer!

III

One more to the point.

There is what is commonly agreed to be a funny proverb which taken literally means: "The burning ghat can be known only if (one) had died previously." It is absurd on the face of it. It is not necessary for one to have died previously to know where the dead bodies are burnt. One passes by the village burning ghat often enough to know where it is. Further, one who dies does not know where he is being taken! So it is impossible for a dead man to know the burning ghat.

A proverb cannot be without meaning; and the meaning

is often hidden in a mystery. This proverb should have its meaning; it cannot be for mere fun.

Now, let us probe a little deeper. "Burning Ghat" represents destruction, or that which burns. The first part of the proverb literally means "At the death of 'before' and 'after' only....." We all know that the first thing that asserts itself in man is 'I' the false ego that arrogates to itself the doership of every action. The next is a natural corollary of the first—the idea of "mineness" which spreads its possessive net over a large field and gets the 'I' itself entangled in its meshes! Every one of the saints and seers of India has declared emphatically that unless this false ego is annihilated in toto a man cannot attain salvation. Whatever path he might follow, this is a condition prerequisite to realisation. All the Tamil Saints of South India have trumpeted this Truth in unmistakable terms; and one has chosen to express it in the form of the proverb! "O fool! Only when the first thing (I) and the later thing (mine) die, can you perceive that Ghat of Knowledge which burns ignorance!" What a sublime thought! And, what a tragic mutilation has it suffered by the passage of time and by falling into the hands of unthinking revellers!

May you all understand the real import of the Great Sayings and imbibe it in your every day life!

Om Santi! Santi!! Santi!!!

THE MAHA KUMBHA MELA

The Maha Kumbha Mela is held once in 12 years at Haridwar, Allahabad, Ujjain and Nasik. This is also called Purna Kumbha Mela. The Ardha (half) Kumbha is celebrated 6 years after the Maha Kumbha. Ther are some fixed days during the period of the Mela for bathing and a bath in the Ganga on those days is considered very sacred and holy. Millions of people assemble here during the sacred Mela Day. Mahavaruni, Navami, Chaturdasi, Amavasya and Poornima are some of the other sacred days during the Mela which lasts for over a month.

Haridwar—its importance.

Hardwar is situated in the Saharanpur district of the Uttar Pradesh at the Northern end of the Sivalik Hills. These hills are among the most ancient rocks of the world and have yielded many relics of the hoary past. Haridwar is on the Dehra Dun line of the East Indian Railway.

It is described as the holy of holies on the sacred banks of the Ganga. Haridwar occurs often in many Puranic texts. It is known also as Mayapuri and Gangawar. History also reveals many interesting details about this holy place.

In the third A.D. Pali historians describe Asoka as having engraved 14 edicts in Haripur, identified with Haridwar. Hieun Tsang, the Chinese traveller who visited India about 630 A.D. wrote about Haridwar as a holy place where lakhs of people had their sacred bath. In 1398 Timur, the lame, overran Haridwar, but in the second half of the 16th century Akbar made amendments for it by abolishing pilgrim taxes. Akbar drank Ganga water every day from sealed vessels.

Ghulam Kadir, helped by a Hindu Minister, looted and destroyed Haridwar in 1786. Under Raja Ummeth Singh, in about 1801, Gurkhas ruled the town and sold their criminals there for prices ranging from Rs, 15/- to 500/-. Half a century later, Haridwar, became part of Queen Victoria's Empire and was "developed under a policy of religious non-interference."

Ganga and Brahma Kund

In ancient days King Bhagiratha of the Ikshwaku line the royal house which Lord Rama belongs to, brought down the Ganga from the Jata (matted locks) of Siva and it was Brahma Kund that the Ganga first touched the earth. The story goes that 60,000 ancestors of King Bhagiratha were reduced to ashes by a Rishi's curse in the nether world, and it was only the waters of Ganga that could bring them back to life. King Bhagiratha by the severest type of austerity for years, propitiated Lord Siva and the Ganga who came down to the earth at last to bless the dead princes with life as also to bestow sacredness on coming generations.

It was at Brahma Kund that King Shweta did severe Tapas to propitiate Brahma, the first progenitor who blessed him saying, "This place will be known after me; and here the trinity Brahma, Vishnu and Siva reside for ever and here Ganga gives humanity the benefit of all the holy waters in India." Not simply for these those lakhs gather there during the Mela at the Brahma Kund. It is to participate in that special sacredness that springs to life at Haridwar once in twelve years on the occasion of the Kumbha Mela.

The most sacred spot in Haridwar is Harkipairi or the Brahama Kund where people have the holy dip. For centuries it continued to be a very sacred spot of religious and spiritual importance. The evening Arati at Hari-ki-pairi is a lovely sight, when devotees send floating down the stream hundreds of lamps.

The main current of the Ganga flows by the side of a blue mountain and is popularly know as the Neeladhara or the blue current. A bath in this main stream, at the Kankhal ghat ends all future births and takes the soul to heaven. Kankhal two miles from Hardwar is the place where Daksha Prajapati performed his famous Yajna. Around Haridwar there are a number of old temples on high hill tops, like Mansa Devi and Chandi Devi temples. There are many Dharmasalas at Haridwar where pilgrims can stay.

Origin and Glory of Kumbha Mela

Once in days of Yore the Devas and the Asuras desirous of partaking the Immortal Nectar churned the ocean named Ksheerodhi with the help of Lord Vishnu, Mandarachala mountain was the churning rod. Vasuki, the king of serpents accepted to be the rope for churning the ocean. As a result of the churning 14 divine things came out of the ocean: and one among them was the nectar. The nectar was preserved in a golden pot (Kumbha or Kalasa). Jayanta, the son of Indra the King of Gods, took the nectar pot and ran away to save it from the demons. When Sukracharya (preceptor of the demons) came to know of this, he told the demons and they chased Jayanta. In the chase and tussle that ensued 12 days passed.

Wherever the demons overtook Jayanta and tried to drink the nectar in all such places Jupiter, Moon, Sun and Saturn saved the nectar from falling into the hands of the demons. Yet the nectar fell down in different places. The places where the nectar dropped down are Haridwar, Ujjain, Nasik and Allahabad. In these places the Kumbha Mela is conducted.

Lord Vishnu appeared and brought peace to one and all by distributing the nectar to deserving people. The Mela comes once in 12 years equivalent to 12 days of the Devas.

When the Jupiter comes to Kumbha Rasi and Sun enters the Mesha Rasi then Kumbha Yoga takes place at Haridwar. This happens once in twelve years.

When Sun enters the Makara Rasi and Jupiter in Mesha Rashi then Kumbha Yoga occurs in Prayag (Allahabad). When the sun enters the Tularasi, when moon and Jupiter happen to be together on Amavasya then is the holy Kumha at Ujjain.

Those who take bath during the Kumbha Parva in the above places derive great benefits. Vishnu Purana says, "A bath in the Ganga on the Kumbha day will give the spiritual benefits of one lac of Pradakshina around the earth." A bath in the Ganga during Kumbha is equal to performance of an Asvamedha sacrifice or giving away in charity one lakh of cows. One Kumbha bath is equal to thousand baths in Kartika month and one hundred baths in Magha and one crore baths in Vaisakhi month.

Purpose of the Mela

In olden days Kumbha Melas were started for the moral and spiritual uplift of the people. Many Mahatmas, sages, Yogins and spiritual preceptors who were practising Tapas and silent meditation in the caves of the Himalayas and forests assembled in these places during Kumbha Mela days for imparting spiritual instructions to the thirsting aspirants and householders. There was not much noise in these days.

People went with Sraddha and Bhava to have Darshan of these Mahatmas and to imbibe the teachings of those highly elevated souls. Religious classes were held, Kathas and discourses were conducted and lectures were delivered by great men of practical experience. Real sincere aspirants were initiated into the mysteries of Yoga and Kaivalya.

Power of congregational Prayer

There is always a mysterious force and power in the collective performance of any act. The efficiency of a Mantra chanted alone is multiplied a hundredfold when articulated enmass by a huge congregation. The mighty car of Jagannath, difficult even for elephants to move, rolls down the street at the united pull of a crowd of devotees. Even so, the thought currents of millions upon millions of faithful devotees by constantly associating through centuries the idea of sanctity and spirituality with particular shrines, places and rivers of this land have created in the latter positive atmosphere of the most powerful spiritualising vibration. When visited with a receptive attitude, even at normal times, such places at once elevate our beings, fill our minds with pure Sattvic feelings and eradicate all impure tendencies. More so, upon special occasions the favourable conjunction of planets adding to this power when countless devotees gather at a given spot with a uniform pious and devoted attitude, a unique spiritual power pervades the whole place.

Lakhs from all over India assemble at this place of pilgrimage to take advantage of the bath in the sacred Ganges at the auspicious moment. Melas and like religious gatherings are specifically meant for the spiritual uplift of the people, When a person has not the leisure to undergo a prolonged course of oral treatment the wise physican gives him a short course of powerful injections with concentrated extracts. This vivifies the person immediately. Similar is the purpose behind attending such occasions whereby thousands who are immersed in secular avocations throughout the year are quickly spiritualised by the subtle Divine presence that permeates the entire place at this time.

Mela Now

What do you find in these days? There will be Bhandara (feasts) everywhere. People are attempting to amass wealth in a variety of ways. They are trying their level best to become rich in a very short time. The sanctity of the functions has vanished. The real spirit is gone. It has become a mere fair. Real, silent Mahatmas do not wish to attend the Mela. The Kumbha Mela or the All-India Religious Conference of a magnanimous sublime nature of yore wherein Rishis, sages and Yogins assembled to exchange their thoughts and spiritual experiences and to disseminate spiritual knowledge to the aspirants and householders at large has now degenerated into a big "Tamasha" or a big fair with tumultuous noise, uproar and merry making. Nowadays there is not much to be seen in the Kumbha Mela except some crowd, noise, dirt, filth, quarrels and fights. The Government has built a separate police station with a reserve police for this purpose. There are many post offices, telegraph offices, and ration depots specially arranged. No religious propaganda can be done. People's minds get restless and agitated in the enormous crowd. They have to wander amidsts all sorts of people and spend sleepless nights with poor accommodation. They undergo a lot of trouble through in factious diseases that are common in all the crowded places. People enjoy some show, colour, sound, blows and then return home with nothing substantial after spending the money in useless directions. Yet millions of people are in anticipation of getting joy, bliss and spiritual benefit by attending the Melas. This is Maya. This is the trick of Maya through the force of curiosity to delude people who have lost their power of discrimination.

To the shop-keepers and hawkers the Mela is a time for making profit. For tricksters and charlatans it is a fertile field for swindling the gullible public and filling their own pockets. To the permanent residents it is a time of great confusion when their peace is disturbed and their systematic routine life is rudely upset. Pleasure lovers and pickpockets find in it scope to ply their shabby profession. To the authorities it is a headache with the constant round of vigilance and control over unruly crowds. Even so, for the sincere and earnest Sadhakas and eager selfless Mahatmas it is a God-given opportunity to respectively receive and to give the precious knowledge of Self. Thus what you derive out of it depends largely on the state and attitude of mind with which you attend the Mela and also the way in which you spend your time in the Mela.

Make the best use of Mela

Though the place may be filled with many sorts of people, yet there are some highly advanced spiritual souls, Mandalesvars and learned Pundits of the Sanatana Dharma Sabha, who untiringly work and clear the doubts of all aspirants and guide them in the spiritual path. They work for the spiritual good of the public. Again in some silent corners you will find some great Virakta Mahatmas and Tyagis. You must hunt out such great souls among the Sadhus, Sannyasins, Yogis and Naga Babas. They will guide you in the right path. Have Darshan of such Mahatmas and get spiritual instructions. Then you will be spiritually benefited.

To take full advantage and derive maximum benefit at these times you must come to the place as a devotee and a pilgrim. You must leave behind all your wealth Abhiman, status Abhiman, caste Abhiman and Babu Abhiman. Maintain a receptive attitude of the mind. Feel that you visit the Divine Presence. Learn to feel the sense of Advaitic equality by moving freely in high and low. Try to behold the Virat form of the Lord in the huge multitude that is present there. Be prepared to endure little hardships and petty inconveniences that are bound to occur. Good and bad are co-existent everywhere. Therefore resolve to see the good and receive the good that you see in the place.

Do not approach with a critical fault-finding mind. Where religious discourses and Upadeshas are given receive them readily. Do not look to the person who gives it. Though there might be all sorts of people yet among them you will find highly advanced, virtuous, spiritual souls also. No not allow your mind to become distracted and restless by the enormous crowd. Have a definite programme of Sadhana. Do plenty of Japa. Study Gita, Upanishads Ramayana and Bhagavat. Have Satsanga with Mahatmas. Observe Mouna. Do plenty of charity. Serve Sadhus and Mahatmas. Approach them with Bhakti and fruits in hand. Pray for spiritual instructions.

When you come to Haridwar for the Kumbha Mela, make it a point to finish some lacs of Japa during these days. Observe Anusthana. Japa done in holy places on such occasions will have marvellous influence and bestow on you spiritual benefits. For 15 or 30 days observe Anusthana. Take milk and fruits only. Do not wander hither and thither. You will grow wonderfully by silent rigid Sadhana. Serve and help the sick persons. There is a very good opportunity for you to do Niskama Karma Yoga. Such kind of spiritual Sadhana must be practised during the Mela which comes once in 12 years. Generally pilgrimages should be performed with the above discipline. Every year people go to Rishikesh and Haridwar, Badrinath and other places. They should all observe the above discipline and then only they would derive the benefits of performing Yatra or pilgrimage.

How to judge a Mahatma

As there is abundant free food for Sadhus and Sannyasins, beggars in orange-robes flock in countless numbers to have an easy comfortable living for six months. Money is simply wasted. Worldly people are deceived. They are not able to find out real spiritual souls. Systematic organised religious preaching muse be done. Then the Kumbha Mela will become a blessing to humanity at large.

Worldly people nowadays entertain foolish ideas about a Mahatma. To deceive them and amass wealth, many people put on gerrua cloth, grow Jata and beards, and young boys and young men throw away their clothes and kowpeen and walk naked in the midst of householders and pose for big Jitendriya Yogis. Many learned men waste their precious time in unnecessary discussions and sectarian quarrels and pass for Jivanmuktas. People should not be carried away by external appearances. They take a physically nude Sadhu for a great Mahatma in the beginning. After a close contact, they lose faith in him. What is wanted is mental nudity, i.e., complete eradication of Vasanas, egoism, etc. Oh dear friends! Do not be deceived by appearances. You cannot study a Mahatma by a simple casual talk for a day or two. You must closely live with him if you want to have a correct inference.

Grihasthis should not put so many questions as to the previous name, caste, creed, qualifications, age, etc., of Sannyasins. They can talk only on philosophical points with a view to clear doubts. Then and then alone they can be benefited by Satsanga of Mahatmas. Satsanga is the easiest and quickest means to change the worldly mind towards the spiritual path and to overhaul thoroughly the vicious and wrong Samskaras. Live in the company of wise Sadhus. The company itself is the spiritual education. Serve them with Bhakti and Sraddha. Attend to their wants. Get Upadesh from them. Then you will have spiritual growth.

May God bless you with more energy to do real sustained solid Sadhana! May God bestow on you joy, peace, bliss and Immortality!

Om Shanti! Shanti!! Shanti!!!

WAKE UP O! MAN

Oh, This is a very beautiful world with gardens,
Picturesque landscape, beautiful wife, wealth,
Car, bungalow, tea, coffee, cocoa, laddus, rasgullas,
Intelligent I.A.S. sons and M.B.B.S. daughters.
O! Man, have you analysed all your experiences?
These are your experience, Pain, sorrow, misery,
        disease, old age and death,
Momentary excitement, momentary sensations of flesh,
Momentary itching and scratching of nerves,
        senses and mind.
But the experience of a life a meditation,
       dispassion and renunciation,
Is freedom, perfection, independence,
      Supreme Peace and Immortal Bliss.
Now at least wake up, O! Man, and realise
      your real essential divine nature.